"Any kind of person can murder... even your grandmother. I know!"

- Bruno Antony in STRANGERS ON A TRAIN

MURDER is SERVED

MURDER is SERVED

Bambi Everson

EVERSON COLEMAN

NEW YORK

CAUTION: Professionals and amateurs are hereby warned that the play represented in this book is subject to a royalty. It is fully protected under the copyright laws of the United States of America, and of all countries covered by the International Copyright Union (including the Dominion of Canada and the rest of the British Commonwealth), and of all countries covered by the Pan-American Copyright Convention and the Universal Copyright Convention, and of all countries with which the United States has reciprocal copyright relations. All rights, including professional, amateur, motion picture, recitation, lecturing, public reading, radio broadcasting, television, video or sound taping, all other forms of mechanical or electronic reproductions, information storage and retrieval systems and photocopying, and the rights of translation into foreign languages, are strictly reserved. Particular emphasis is laid upon the question of public readings, permission for which must be secured from the Author or their authorized representative. We'll probably say yes, but please ask.

Exceptions are made in the case of brief quotations embodied in critical reviews, educational or scholarly purposes and certain artistic and other noncommercial uses permitted by copyright law. This is a work of fiction. Any resemblance to actual events or persons, living or dead, is entirely coincidental.

All inquiries concerning rights should be sent via email to bambieverson@gmail.com.

For performance of any music, songs, arrangements, and recordings mentioned in this volume that are protected by copyright, the permission of the copyright owners must be obtained; or other songs and recordings in the public domain substituted.

Copyright © 2020 Bambi Everson

Editing, cover art and layout by Frank Coleman
Published by Everson/Coleman

First Edition: September 2022

All rights reserved.

ISBN: 978-1-7375411-7-2

AUTHOR'S NOTE

This may have been my favorite play to write, as I had a wonderful inspiration for the lead character, my own dear mother. I once had the misfortune, or maybe luck as it turned out, to witness my mother playing scrabble with her then-husband, Jerry. My mother is a terrible speller, so the game quickly devolved, with poor Jerry being pelted with not only scrabble letters, but anything else that was handy. Mom was in my head throughout the writing process, and she was delighted to be the cover girl for the book, stating that she was finally getting the 15 minutes of fame unjustly denied her thus far.

I always knew I wanted the superb Wynne Anders to play Rita. When she did, at the Emerging Artists Theatre New Works series, my friends in the audience wanted to know how she had channeled my mother so perfectly without ever meeting her.

I also wanted to write for women of a certain age, as I was finding precious little available with older people as lead characters that weren't dead, or dying, or cantankerous comic relief – albeit, my mother often fell into the latter category. My mother was very outspoken about her sexual exploits when she was in her late 70s, much to my chagrin, but I wanted to add that to the character.

Finding the other actors was sheer serendipity. Wynne introduced me to the lovely Vivian Meisner, who counterbalanced Rita's character beautifully with her soft spoken, gentle manner. Seeing them work with and off each other was pure theater magic.

Dave Mazzeo had played an older gentleman in a short play of mine called MEETING MERVYN. He brought the house down with his quiet, humorous manner. I wrote MURDER IS SERVED with him in mind even though he is far from the repressed, bullied Steve in the play. Wynne and Dave have remarkable improvisational instincts, and played off each other brilliantly, even with a distinct lack of rehearsal time. I am forever grateful to them both.

When it came to having a detective, I was lucky enough to see it many different ways. One of my core actors, Keith Panzarella, gave it a shot as a young, headstrong, ambitious detective. Always a pleasure to work with him.

At the New Works series, my partner-in-crime, Frank Coleman, took over the role as a weary detective, almost ready for retirement, resentful at having to work a case so early in the morning. We had to change a couple of lines, as my darling Frank would never be mistaken for a young Russell Crowe, whereas Keith might be.

I always thought the detective was the least exciting role in the play, but when I saw a staged reading at The Little Theatre of Alexandria, Virginia, I was surprised how the actor found so many places for laugh lines, and I realized it was a role anyone could make their own.

Of all my plays, MURDER IS SERVED has seen the most traction thus far, having been performed in the aforementioned Little Theater, and on a tour of senior homes with the Atlanta-To-Go theater company!

I was able to expand the play for the touring company, adding an additional scene for Steve and Maude, which I think enhances it.

I hope to see a full production of it somewhere, as it does have a very special place in my heart. Plays are meant to be seen, but I do hope it's still an enjoyable read, and I thank you from the bottom of my cold dark heart for all the support.

And thanks, Mom, for being you.

Bambi Everson
New York City, August 2022

PRODUCTION HISTORY

Reading – A/R/T NY, NYC, 2017
With Wynne Anders*, Dave Mazzeo*, Vivian Meisner*, Keith Panzarella, and Sarah Gaines (stage directions)

Staged reading – Emerging Artists Theatre, NYC, 2017
With Wynne Anders*, Dave Mazzeo*, Vivian Meisner*, and Frank Coleman*

Staged reading –The Little Theatre of Alexandria, VA, 2019
One Act Competition, 2nd Place

Touring production – Atlanta Theatre-To-Go, 2021
Regional senior homes and centers

* appearing with permission of Actors' Equity Association.

Poster for Emerging Artists Theatre (EAT). Graphics by Frank Coleman

At A/R/T NY: Bambi Everson, Dave Mazzeo, Sarah Gaines, Wynne Anders, Vivian Meisner, Keith Panzarella (l to r). Photo: Frank Coleman.

Wynne Anders, Frank Coleman, Vivian Meisner, and Dave Mazzeo (l to r) at EAT.

Dave Mazzeo, Wynne Anders at Emerging Artists Theatre (EAT). Photo: Bambi Everson.

MURDER IS SERVED at The Little Theatre of Alexandria, VA

ATLANTA THEATER-TO-GO
Reprinted from Dramatists Guild Magazine, May 2022

Anytime a playwright's work is chosen, especially mine, it is a thrill. MURDER IS SERVED has always had a special place in my heart. I wanted to write a play for strong, viable elders, still having and enjoying romantic encounters.

I based the lead character, Rita, on my mother and wondered if people who didn't know my mother would believe the character with all her eccentricities. Both Rita and my mother are a bit extreme.

When Atlanta Theatre-To-Go wrote and told me of their plans to take this short piece to senior homes around Atlanta, I was excited but also worried. Would a play about a love triangle among octogenarians in a rehab center, possibly resulting in murder, be appropriate for seniors living in a similar situation? Would the humor come through? In early discussions with the director, it was important that no character be played for pity. Here are three people in their 80s having a crisis, but they are sharp and capable of both love and calculated deception. We had to make some slight adjustments for the sake of the intended audience. Rita, like my mother, cursed like a sailor. The company wanted to tone down her dialogue. I agreed, as long as the intent remained clear.

Since I live in NYC, I wasn't able to see the production, but I'm sure the director handled it well. The rules of the Dramatists Guild are such that you can't change the words without the express permission of the playwright, but I certainly did not want to offend groups of senior citizens.

The most exciting thing was they asked me to extend the play so it could run as a standalone. Delving into these characters after a few years was both a challenge and a delight. I always intended to write more for Maud, the love interest. I thought a late-night geriatric balcony scene might work, since Rita had already taken away her husband Steve's phone.

Looking at the photos that the company sent me, it looked like it played well, and I am eager to hear the play again with the new added scene.

Of course, for me, the most important thing is that everyone has a good time: the audience, the actors, and the crew. Especially in these darker times, we need a respite from the toils of the world. We need to laugh, to escape at least for an hour. Atlanta Theatre-To-Go kept me smiling with their Instagram posts, photos, and comments about their experience.

I learn so much as a playwright by seeing where the laughs are, and if they are consistent no matter who is saying them, or where they are being played. I was so grateful that the company considered this tour a success.

Bambi Everson
New York City, April 2022

Atlanta Theater-To-Go production of MURDER IS SERVED

MURDER IS SERVED
By Bambi Everson
One act, approximately 45 minutes

CHARACTERS:

RITA LOWENTHAL (83) Strident, tactless and high-strung.
STEVE LOWENTHAL (90) Long-suffering second husband to Rita.
MAUDE ELLIOT (84) Quintessential nurturing grandmother.
DETECTIVE ROBERT BAILEY (age unspecified) Seasoned professional.

SETTING: Modest home in California.
TIME: The present.

SYNOPSIS: A murderous love triangle amongst octogenarians in an assisted living facility. Married for 40 years, Steve Lowenthal's life has been made intolerable by his henpecking wife, Rita. Finding new love in the rehabilitation center leads to deceit, treachery, revenge and cheating at Scrabble.

PRODUCTION NOTE: You can use brightly colored play-dough for Rita's Christmas candies. It should look hideous.

Special thanks to Paul Adams and company at Emerging Artists Theater.

SCENE 1

RITA and STEVE's kitchen table. It is cluttered from years of living. STEVE and RITA are playing Scrabble, as they have done for years. RITA is an aggressive player. STEVE clearly has something on his mind.

RITA
Go!!

STEVE
Can we put this in hold for a while? We really need to talk.

RITA
Typical. You always want to stop when you're ahead. You're trying to break my concentration. Not happening! It's your move, so go!

STEVE
(sighs)
Fine. "Proctors." 19 points.

RITA
What is a proctor? Is that an ass doctor? I'm getting the book.

STEVE
A proctor. Someone who watches a person during an exam. Plural. There were 7 proctors at the SAT exam. I think I get an extra 50 for using all my letters, right?

RITA
Goddamn it!! 69 points! Fine!

STEVE
It doesn't make much difference at this point, but the c is on a double word score. So, it's actually 88...

RITA
Goddamn it!!!

STEVE
Let's just call it a night. You're getting yourself all worked up, and frankly, I'm really not having much fun.

RITA
Do you want a drink?

STEVE
Sure. Maybe that will help. A nice glass of Ovaltine. Thanks!

RITA
I'm not getting it. You get it. After you pick your letters. I can't trust you if my back is turned.

STEVE
(taking his letters)
I have never cheated at Scrabble. There. Happy?

Gets up from table to make Ovaltine. He is slow and shuffles over.

STEVE
You want something?

RITA
Shhhh! I'm thinking. Yeah, bring me a root beer. And some of those fudge cookies. And don't spill anything. Goddamn crappy letters.

STEVE returns with her root beer and his Ovaltine.

RITA
Dump, triple letter score. 18. Where are the goddamn cookies?

STEVE
Sorry.

Gets back up to get cookies. Meanwhile, RITA sneaks a peek at his letters. She seems satisfied.

RITA
You have a mind like a sieve!

STEVE
I don't know how you put up with me.

STEVE starts studying his scrabble letters and board.

RITA
It's not easy, believe me. Go! We haven't got all night.

STEVE
We don't?

RITA
Oh, my God! I told you. I have to decorate for my folk dancing group.

STEVE
Right! Ok, not much here, so... S-T-E-R. Dumpster 3, 4, 7, 13, 14, 15, double letter 17 points.

RITA
I hate it when you add on to my words!

STEVE
It's allowed, right?

RITA
Yes. It's allowed. It's just annoying. Ha! On your R, a, v, e, n. 8, double word 16.

STEVE
Good one.

RITA
Don't patronize me. Your move.

STEVE
G, o, a, on the T, e and your other e - goatee.

RITA
Dammit, dammit, dammit!

STEVE
I can't do this anymore.

RITA
Fine!

Throws the Scrabble bag at him, tips over the board.

RITA
You clean it up then! I'm going to change for dance.

STEVE
Doesn't it start at eight?

RITA
I have to set up chairs. And decorate. I have a lot of responsibility. You would know that, if you ever came with me.

STEVE
It's just not my thing. The music is always so loud.

RITA
That's because some of us don't like to wear our hearing aids. Especially Manny, the sound guy. No one is complaining, though. You need to get out of the house more. Dancing is good for your heart.

STEVE
I have arthritis in both knees. And you always kick me if I'm not moving fast enough. I'd rather go to a nice movie. Couldn't we just do that tonight? There is a silent movie festival at the Paramount. Douglas Fairbanks.

RITA
NO! I have dance. Oh, I should have married Arthur Wisenbaum. Now he knew how to have a good time.

STEVE
He's dead.

RITA
Well, he'd still be more fun than you.

STEVE
Can you just sit for a moment?

RITA
I was sitting. If I am late, the chairs will not be set up properly.

STEVE
You have never been late for anything in 36 years. You just wind up sitting in the parking lot for two hours.

RITA
That's because I need the best spot.

STEVE
Please. Just five minutes.

RITA
Go!

STEVE
Sitting, please. Put your phone down.

RITA
No. You said five minutes. You now have four minutes and 48 seconds. You are wasting time.

STEVE
This is hard with you looking at a stopwatch... I think I need to leave.

RITA
Well, hurry up then. You can't be seen wearing that. If I'm driving you, we have to leave NOW.

STEVE
Rita, I'm not leaving with you. I am leaving without you.

RITA
Ha. You never go anywhere without me.

STEVE
Actually, That's not true. This is really hard. I have been seeing someone else.

RITA
That's ridiculous! Who? The cleaning lady? I never did trust that woman. I think she's been stealing my marijuana gummy worms!

STEVE
Her name is Maude. I met her in my PT group. She had cataract surgery, and a hip replacement.

RITA
So, she's blind? Well, that makes sense. I doubt she'll stick around once she regains her eyesight. You're not exactly Paul Newman, you know.

STEVE
Newman is dead. I told her I look like Milton Berle gone to seed. But it's not like that. Maude is quiet. A homebody. Bakes cookies.

RITA
So how old is Donna Reed?

STEVE
Maude will be 84 in February.

RITA
I'm 83!! How will I explain to my friends that you left me for an older woman? A blind cripple, at that! How will I live that down? I am not a toaster that you can return to Walmart.

STEVE
You are not a toaster. I am not trading you in for another model. But Rita, you can't possibly be happy living like this. You see me as an albatross. A cross to bear.

RITA
My albatross! My cross-eyed bear! Who are you to question my happiness? This is me happy. I have been fucking happy for 36 fucking years. You can't toss a person away like garbage. Garbage collection is on Tuesdays and Thursdays. Do you want me to just sit there and wait for the truck?

STEVE
Don't you think we both deserve a little peace and quiet? After all this time, don't you think we could use a little rest?

RITA
I'll rest when I'm dead! Does she – this person – know your schlong hasn't worked in years? Does she know it needs to be wrapped in papier-mâché and propped up with duct tape? And that barely works because you have to pee as soon as the cast dries?

STEVE
It's not about that. It's about companionship. It's about going gently into that dark night.

RITA
Get in the car. I have to go to dance. I am not discussing this anymore.

STEVE
Please. I'd rather just stay home. I promise I'll watch a movie and we can talk when you get home.

RITA
Fine, but give me your cell phone.

STEVE
Why?

RITA
I don't want you having phone sex with Helen Keller while I'm gone.

STEVE
That doesn't make sense. Helen Keller wouldn't have a phone. What if there's an emergency?

RITA
Guess you should have thought of that before you became a geriatric Valentino!

She grabs the phone. She steps on a scrabble piece.

RITA
DAMMIT!
(picking up the scrabble pieces and throwing them at him)
Damn you! I'll be home by ten.

RITA exits slamming the door hard! STEVE slowly and carefully puts all the scrabble pieces back in the box and then tosses the box in the trash.

STEVE
Finish – 4, 5, 6, 7, 8, 12, double word 24. Game over.

BLACKOUT

SCENE 2

Outside Brookfield Convalescent Hospital. STEVE is on a patio looking up at a window. He's not sure what to do. He tries to throw a pebble at the window, but it throws his back out. He is in pain, but tries again and again. Finally, a figure comes to the window. It is MAUDE ELLIOT, in her nightgown and walker. She has a patch over one eye. She opens the window at exactly the wrong moment and is almost hit with a pebble.

MAUDE
What on Earth?

STEVE
Sorry! So sorry. Maude... Maude... Down here!

MAUDE
Who's there? I almost lost an eye!

STEVE
It's Steve.

MAUDE
Who?

STEVE
Steve. I'm down here.

MAUDE
I can't see you. Let me get my glasses.

MAUDE goes off and comes back, wearing glasses over her eye patch.

MAUDE
Nope. No good. Can't see a darn thing. I thought there was a hailstorm. Where are you? Say something, so I know it's you.

STEVE
Tomorrow, the birds will sing. You can see now?

MAUDE
Oh. "City Lights." One of my favorites.

STEVE
Mine, too. It's playing tonight. I wish we could go.

MAUDE
Haven't you seen it before?

STEVE
Dozens of times. But never with you.

MAUDE
Maybe next time. I'm at the mercy of Brookfield doctors for a few more days. Why are you here?

STEVE
I have to talk to you.

MAUDE
I don't know if you are aware, but there is a modern invention now called the telephone.

STEVE
Don't have it. Long story. Can you come down?

MAUDE
It's after hours. The front door is locked. I'm in my jammies. It takes me 20 minutes to get dressed these days.

STEVE
You look beautiful just as you are. Would the doorman let you out for some air?

MAUDE
With all that gravel? I might break my other hip.

STEVE
Then the geriatric balcony scene it is.

MAUDE
I wish I could see you better. I'm afraid if I lean out any further, I'll lose my balance! Six months in a body cast if I survived! Can't this wait 'til tomorrow? We have the sing-along at two. I could easily slip away after. What time is your PT?

STEVE
I can't keep this inside anymore. I love you, Maude!

MAUDE
What? Sorry... Maybe I should turn up my hearing aid.

STEVE
I said, I love you! It was never my plan, but I love every single thing about you!

MAUDE
Did I hear right? Love? Are you sure?

STEVE
Sure as shootin'. I know it's fast, but at our age, one has to move quickly before the end credits roll.

MAUDE
We hardly know each other!

STEVE
I know everything I need to know about you. You have a voice like an angel. You are kind and compassionate. Intelligent, well read...

MAUDE
I thought it was my rocking body.

STEVE
That, too! You are a pretty snappy looking dish.

MAUDE
And you are my Valentino. But my mama always told me not to get attached to something that isn't mine. I have always respected the institution of marriage.

STEVE
Who wants to live in an institution? Look, I am not some cad who speaks ill of his wife.

MAUDE
I know. She can't be all bad. No one is.

STEVE
Well, she comes the closest. Just tell me you feel the same.

MAUDE
I felt it the moment we started talking.

STEVE
That's all I needed to hear. A thousand goodnights, dear Maude.

MAUDE
'Til tomorrow, my love. Be careful.

STEVE
It's too late to be careful, too late to be sensible. I'm throwing caution to the wind.

STEVE trips over something.

STEVE
OOF! Who the heck puts a bench in the driveway?

MAUDE
That's not the driveway. The parking lot is to the left. Are you ok? How did you even get up here?

STEVE
On love's light wings, did I scour these walls and... I have a key to the garage.

MAUDE
You'd better go. You don't want to get charged with trespassing.

STEVE
Tomorrow, then?

MAUDE
Yes. Tomorrow.

STEVE
And if the spirits are willing, all the days to come.

STEVE blows kisses, and like a stealth ninja fumbles his way out of the patio.

END OF SCENE

SCENE 3

The next morning. RITA is at the kitchen table, whistling. She is making Christmas candy. STEVE enters. He looks exhausted.

STEVE
It's 6:45. How long have you been up?

RITA
Since 5. I wanted to get a head start on my Christmas candy. I have a lot of people on my list this year.

STEVE
You are pretty chipper this morning.

RITA
I have always been a morning person. You know that. I get up and get going.

STEVE
Is there any coffee?

RITA
Oh, I forgot. Just turn on the coffee maker. Yesterday's will heat up. Oh, my green marzipans look so cute. Like little limes. Here, taste one.

STEVE
No, that's ok. You look like you are on a roll.

RITA
Oh, I am. Red strawberries, green limes, yellow lemons, orange oranges, and blue... well they are bigger than berries, so I guess they are just blue balls. This year, they are going to be better than ever.

STEVE
How was dance?

RITA
Great! Morris Sternberg said he never saw anyone rock The Salty Dog Rag like I do. I think he's got the hots for me, but he's temporarily married.

STEVE
Temporarily?

RITA
Agnes had a stroke last year. She's in hospice.

STEVE
Well, nice to know you are exploring your options.
(pause)
About last night...

RITA
I don't know why I got so upset about things. Lots of men still find me attractive. My boobs are perky like a 30-year-old's. I have more energy than my kids. My son adores me. One phone call, and he'll pay for me to come to NY and live with him and Stephanie. I have grandkids who adore me. They always tell me I am way more fun than their other grandparents.

STEVE
All the other grandparents are dead.

RITA
That's irrelevant. I am not a used car, ready for the junkyard.

STEVE
Of course not. I never implied...

RITA
Personally, I don't think you and your little floozy will last. But go ahead and have your end-of-life crisis. Lord knows, I had my share of indiscretions.

STEVE
You have?

RITA
You were always so naive. I always had a voracious appetite. Remember Pablo? Ever wonder why I never learned Flamenco dancing? And Juan? Mandolin lessons? You never heard me practice, did you?

STEVE
That mandolin was expensive!

RITA
It's still in the hall closet. I can't even look at it since Juan had that boating accident.

STEVE
What?

RITA
He lost both his arms. He's at the Jewish home, learning to paint with his toes.

STEVE
I had no idea. None at all.

RITA
I always told you – you needed to get out more. Remember Saul, the usher at the Rialto? I still get in there for free. Then there was Myron and Byron, those twins at the 7-11. And Martha, but that was just an experiment. The point is – I always came back to you. Despite all your obvious flaws, I do love you, you flatulent meathead. Here.

Packs up a baggie of marzipan and hands it to him.

RITA
You'll need the sugar rush if you have PT. You didn't eat breakfast. The Access-a-Ride should be here any minute.

STEVE
You're not going to come with me?

RITA
Oh, good lord, no! I have all these candies to pack up and send out.

STEVE
You really should ease up on those. It's an awful lot of work, and frankly...

RITA
Are you kidding me?? People expect them. I have been making these candies for over 40 years.

STEVE
(pouring himself a cup of coffee)
Maybe I should just stay home today. There has been a lot of information to assimilate here. For both of us. We have to think about what we are going to do.

RITA
Do? We are not going to do anything. You are going to PT. If you have a fling with Mrs. Methuselah, I hope she has a nice house. And cooks with a lot of salt. I'll be right here. For now. Unless Morris Sternberg has an opening.

A car horn beeps outside.

RITA
That will be your ride. Don't let that nurse go easy on you. You can bump that treadmill up to four, at least. You are tougher than they think.

STEVE
I could say the same for you. Ok, then. Back in a couple hours. Dinner?

RITA
I am going to be pretty busy with this. I'll order Mexican.

STEVE
I don't really like– That will be fine.

RITA
See ya!!

RITA returns to rolling up and bagging up her marzipan candies. She is whistling.

BLACKOUT

SCENE 4

The hospital PT Room. MAUDE is sitting in a wheelchair. One eye is bandaged. STEVE walks up behind her and kisses her gently on the top of her head.

MAUDE
Steve, is that you?

STEVE
Of course, it's me! How many other men are kissing you?

MAUDE
I have no idea. Every time I say, "Steve, is that you?" They always say, "Yes." But it never sounds exactly like you. Were you trying to fool me with that Russian accent? It's very sexy.

STEVE
Maude! You have to be careful. There are some very unscrupulous characters around here.

MAUDE
(laughs)
You silly. I only have eye for you.

They kiss tenderly.

MAUDE
How did things go at home? I see you are still in one piece. So, either you didn't tell her, or...

STEVE
I did tell her.

MAUDE
And?

STEVE
Well, at first, she was mad. Fighting mad.

MAUDE
Understandably.

STEVE
But today, she was strangely calm. Either she was ok with it, or she didn't believe me. I tend to think it's the latter. Rita is not one to surrender graciously.

MAUDE
Maybe we should rethink this. I am not a home wrecker. I never have been. There are some boundaries I will never cross, even at this stage of the game.

STEVE
My home has been wrecked for the past 30 years. You have no idea what I've been through.

MAUDE
I think I have some idea. No marriage is all roses and sunshine. I don't want to give you up, either, but I don't feel right about being the cause of another woman's unhappiness.

STEVE
I think I am the cause of her unhappiness. I am sure she thought she was marrying up after her first divorce. I think, ultimately, I must have been a bit of a disappointment to her. I know I wasn't ready to get married again, but "no" is just not in Rita's vocabulary. She swooped in, like the flock of crows in "The Birds," right after the funeral. She preyed on my loneliness and my vulnerability. Elizabeth, my first wife, had been sick for so long. It was all about making her happy in the time we had left. In those last few months, dementia had set in. Harder for me than her. She thought she was in an all-girls Catholic school in the '40s. She was always concerned that the Mother Superior would catch us together, and she would get expelled.

MAUDE
That's rather sweet.

STEVE
It was until she noticed how old I was. Then she was convinced she was being molested by Cardinal Spellman, and kept reporting me to the police.

MAUDE
Shortly before my husband passed away, he accused me of plotting to kill Joan Crawford. He thought I was Gloria Grahame in "Sudden Fear."

STEVE
I see the resemblance.

MAUDE
Did Nurse Ratchet put you through the wringer yet?

STEVE
Yup. I'm good to go. Except I'd rather stay. Do you need anything from the outside world?

MAUDE
Only you.

STEVE bends down to hug her. MAUDE puts her arms around his waist and feels something in his jacket pocket.

MAUDE
Is that a bag of marbles in your pocket, or are you just happy to see me?

STEVE
What? Oh, these...
(pulls out bag of marzipan candy)
It's Rita's Christmas candy. Awful stuff. She's been making Marzipan for years. Tastes like wall paste and rubber cement. I am sure nobody likes them, but no one has the heart to tell her.

MAUDE
I love marzipan.

STEVE
Trust me. You wouldn't like these.

MAUDE
Got to be better than those sugar-free, flavor-free, cardboard biscuits they pass off as cookies.

STEVE
(handing her the bag)
Here. You're welcome to them. Don't say I didn't warn you.

MAUDE
What would you like to do now? Maybe a game of Scrabble?

STEVE
Anything but that! May I wheel you to your room?

MAUDE
What would Emily Post say about a married man coming into a lady's hospital room unattended?

STEVE
I think Emily Post knows that there is just so much happiness to go around. If some comes your way, you've got to grab it and hold tight.

MAUDE
I don't think housekeeping has made up the bed yet.

STEVE
(kissing her gently)
We'll figure out something.

BLACKOUT

SCENE 5

The next morning. RITA is alone in the kitchen. She is pacing, worried. She is trying to make breakfast, but something is on her mind. She can't concentrate. She crosses to the coffee maker to pour herself some coffee. She does not see STEVE enter the kitchen.

STEVE
Is the coffee fresh?

RITA screams!

RITA
What are you doing here?

STEVE
I live here.

RITA
You didn't come home for dinner. I was... I was worried sick. I called the hospital. The nurse said you'd left. Where were you?

STEVE
I'm sorry. I was home by eight. You were sleeping so I went into the guest room. I didn't want to wake you.

RITA
Well, you should have left me a note or something. Or called.

STEVE
You had my phone, remember?

RITA
Were you with her?

STEVE
For a little while. I went by the Pantages. They were showing "City Lights."

RITA
You've seen that like a hundred times.

STEVE
It's my favorite.

RITA
So, what did you eat?

STEVE
Oh, I picked up a sandwich at Lemmy's.

RITA
No. At the movies.

STEVE
Oh. Nothing.

RITA
Not even the candy I gave you?

STEVE
Oh, that. Yes. It was delicious.

RITA
Really? You ate that whole bag? How are you feeling?

STEVE
You gave me so many. I shared a couple with the nurses at the hospital.

RITA
You did what? Those were for you. Well... now you've spoiled the surprise. I had little baskets made up for all of them.

STEVE
One less thing for you to worry about. You going to drink that coffee?

RITA
Why? You want some?

STEVE
If you don't mind. And some toast. My tummy's a little off this morning.

RITA
Be my guest. There's lingonberry jam in the fridge.

The doorbell rings.

RITA
You expecting something?

STEVE shakes his head.

RITA
Coming. Who is it?

DETECTIVE
(from outside)
Detective Bailey from the 14th precinct.

RITA
Got any ID?

DETECTIVE shows his ID.

RITA
I can't see that. Slip it through the door.

RITA opens the door a crack and the DETECTIVE slips his ID through the door. RITA slams the door shut quickly.

RITA
Hmmmm. You don't exactly look like your picture. This picture looks like Russell Crowe. And NOT during his Gladiator period.

DETECTIVE
I've been on the force for nine years. I should update the picture. Look, you can call the precinct if you want... Um... I need the ID back, though.

RITA
When I'm finished. Hey Steve, do you know a Detective Bailey?

STEVE
For heaven's sake, Rita. Let the man in.

STEVE goes to the door. RITA grabs her cell phone and exits with the ID in her hand.

STEVE
I'm sorry, sir. My wife is a little high strung.

RITA
(from offstage)
I AM NOT HIGH STRUNG!

DETECTIVE
Is this the home of Steve Lowenthal?

STEVE
Yes. Please come in. Can I offer you something? Coffee? Rita just made a fresh pot.

DETECTIVE
No, thank you. I'm fine. This shouldn't take long.

RITA returns.

RITA
I spoke to your superior.

DETECTIVE
Captain MacCready?

RITA
Yeah. That's him. I guess your eyes really are blue.
(hands back his ID)
If this is about those parking tickets, It's Steve's fault. We should have handicap stickers on both cars.

DETECTIVE
No, Ma'am. You are Mrs. Lowenthal?

RITA
For the time being, anyway. Call me Rita.

DETECTIVE
Maybe I could speak to your husband alone for a few minutes.

RITA
My husband has a mind like a sieve. He gets very confused. He needs me here.

STEVE
It's fine, Officer.

RITA
(to STEVE, correcting him)
Detective!
(to DETECTIVE)
See, I told you. Hopeless! So, Detective...
(looks at ID)
...Bailey, what can we do for you?
(hands back ID, smiling)

DETECTIVE
I am here regarding Maude Elliot. Do you know her?

STEVE
Maude?

RITA
Maude? Like from the TV show? That Bea Arthur was so obnoxious.

STEVE
Rita, stop. Of course I know her, officer. We are both at the Brookfield Convalescent Hospital. She is there full time. I live here. Obviously.

RITA
Maude! Right. The little old lady from Pasadena. What is she complaining about? Whatever it is, she is probably lying.

DETECTIVE
She's not complaining about anything. She's dead.

STEVE
WHAT?? When did this happen?

DETECTIVE
She was found in her room this morning.

STEVE
Heart attack?

DETECTIVE
That's what we thought, at first.

RITA
Well, she was older than God.

DETECTIVE
So, you do know her?

RITA
I only know she was older than me. I never met her.

STEVE
Poor Maude! I hope she didn't suffer.

DETECTIVE
Your name was first in her cell phone. The nurse at the hospital said you were close.

STEVE
We were. I am in shock. Her heart was fine as far as I knew. She was there for a hip replacement and cataract surgery.

DETECTIVE
I don't want to alarm you prematurely, and of course, we need to wait for the full autopsy report, but it does appear Ms. Elliot did not die of natural causes.

STEVE
That's absurd. Maude was the sweetest person on earth. She didn't have an enemy in the world.

RITA
That he knows of. These quiet ones have secrets. We all have secrets - right, Detective?

DETECTIVE
Some more than others. Did you dine at home last night, Mr. Lowenthal?

STEVE
Not last night. I know Tuesday at Brookfield is pot roast, instant mashed potatoes, corn and peas, two bite size cookies for dessert, and apple juice.

RITA
That, you can remember? Honestly, Detective, he forgets where he lives half the time. He hasn't remembered a birthday or anniversary in years!

DETECTIVE
So, you were home?

RITA
Yes.

STEVE
No. I was at the movies. I am sure I still have the ticket stub.

DETECTIVE
That would be helpful.

STEVE goes off to look for it.

DETECTIVE
Why did you say your husband was at home?

RITA
Home, not home. It's the same to me. After 30 years, you get accustomed to sharing the same cage, you know?

The two stand around awkwardly for a moment. STEVE returns.

STEVE
Here you are, Officer.

RITA
Detective!

RITA smiles at the detective.

STEVE
I went to the 6:40 show. Rita was asleep when I returned. I watched the news at 10. Horrible about that accident on the I-40. I ate some cheese and crackers and was asleep myself by 10:30.

RITA
So, that's where the cheese went.

DETECTIVE
Well, everything seems to be in order. I am very sorry about your friend. Please take my card. If you can think of anything at all...

RITA
Like what?

DETECTIVE
Like anyone who might have a reason to harm her, someone who might have benefited from her death.

STEVE
Of course, Offic– Er ...Detective. Anything I can do to help. About the services... I'd like to contribute...

DETECTIVE
I am sure the hospital will be in touch. The Brookfield staff is very concerned. If it turns out she was poisoned, accidentally or not, the hospital staff is liable. The patients are not allowed outside food.

STEVE
I understand.

DETECTIVE
Thank you for your time.

RITA
Would you like some candy for the road?

Hands him a baggie of marzipan fruits.

DETECTIVE
Better not. The wife is after me to cut down on sweets. Take care you two. I'll be in touch.

DETECTIVE exits. RITA is staring at STEVE. After a long pause...

STEVE
What?

RITA
Awful, isn't it?

STEVE
Unbelievable.

RITA
Eat some candy.

Hands him the baggie.

STEVE
No thanks.

RITA
I said, eat some. Here!

STEVE
I... I... have to make some phone calls. How can you think of food at a time like this?

RITA
'Cause you didn't eat these yesterday.

STEVE
So?

RITA
It was just supposed to make you a little sick.

STEVE
What are you talking about?

RITA
Did you give those fucking candies to what's her name, or not?

STEVE
Ok. I did.

RITA
Then we need to get the fuck out of here.

STEVE
What are you saying? What did you do?

RITA
I only put a little in. Just enough for some serious puking and diarrhea.

STEVE
A little what?

RITA
Arsenic trioxide.

STEVE
Rat poison?

RITA
Just a little.

STEVE
Are you kidding me? You killed Maude?

RITA
Well, technically, you killed her. You gave them to her.

STEVE
You are insane! That's like saying the person who ate the tainted Tylenols died by suicide. You poisoned her!

RITA
It will only be traced back to you if they find those candies. Good thing that detective didn't take these. But if he puts 2 and 2 together...

STEVE
We have to call the police now!

RITA
It was an accident. Honestly, she would have had to have eaten the whole bag. Who binge eats marzipan? Anyway... What's done cannot be undone.

STEVE
Now you're Lady Macbeth? Rita, you're not right in the head. Ok. It was an accident. It was intended for me. I am still grappling with that, but it's still a sin to kill someone, last time I checked. Sins have a way of staying with you. Neither one of us could live with that guilt!

RITA
Speak for yourself. Here's why you are not calling the police. One – It's my word against yours. Two – All the other candy is fine. See?
(she pops one into her mouth)
Three – I injected it with one of your insulin hypodermics that I may or may not have hidden among your toiletries. I can keep going.

STEVE
Why? Why would you want to do this?

RITA
I don't get left Steve. I do the leaving. I figured you'd get plenty sick, and crap and puke all over Maude, which would probably take the romance out of your little dalliance. You'd come home stinky and ashamed, and I'd take care of you. You'd be grateful, and things would just continue as they had been before.

STEVE
Before what? Our marriage was over long before you became Lucrezia Borgia. I am calling that detective.

RITA
Hey... a husband can't testify against his wife, right? That's still a thing, isn't it? Marriage is forever. Like cement. Face it. We are embedded. You blow a whistle on me, I let loose on your son's dirty little secret.

STEVE
Leave my son out of this! That was years ago.

RITA
Is there a statute of limitations on embezzlement? I could also say "Oh, how dreadful, Detective! My husband must have killed that poor woman. He hasn't been himself lately." Maybe you'd both wind up in the same prison.

STEVE
Maybe a prison with bars will be safer than the prison I'm in now.

RITA
Really? Is that where you want to spend your final years? With your grandchildren visiting you behind a glass partition? Next to child molesters, men that murder sweet old ladies are prime rib. Everyone had a mother or a grandmother. My guess is, you wouldn't last a month before some prison wolf shanked you in the shower.

STEVE
When did you become this woman? You'll never get away with it.

RITA
We'll see. First things first.

RITA scoops up the remainder of the marzipan candy and takes it outside to the garbage. Then she gets some bleach and starts wiping the counter. STEVE stands in stunned silence, watching her.

RITA
Why don't you make yourself useful? Put on some water for tea.

STEVE
Rita, please, I can't be complicit in this.

RITA
I am afraid you have no choice. I never met the woman. But maybe... maybe... she was putting pressure on you to leave your wife. Maybe she was threatening to sing like a canary... Maybe she left you money in her will... the possibilities are endless.

STEVE is making tea. He reaches into the cupboard. We cannot see what he is doing.

STEVE
Let's just try to think this through rationally. I am sorry I put you in this position in the first place. I am sorry we both were so hopelessly unhappy. I should have done the morally responsible thing, and left before allowing myself to get emotionally attached to another person.

RITA
I never would have let you leave.

STEVE
Maybe. Maybe not. Maybe Irving Mendelbaum could have given you a better life.

RITA
Irving Mendelbaum died four years ago!

RITA sits. STEVE pours them both a cup of tea.

RITA
I still think the obvious thing is to pack up and leave. Somewhere no one would look. Ten Sleep, Wyoming. Or Trenton. You've got savings. After

RITA (cont.)
a few years, we can tell the kids where we are, and this will have all blown over.

STEVE
We didn't get along in a beautiful house surrounded by friends and family. You think things would be better as fugitives in a trailer park? A geriatric Bonnie and Clyde?

RITA
Don't you think it might be kind of romantic? It's a fresh start. I'll dye my hair and you can grow a beard.

STEVE
And where would they send my social security checks? How would I have access to my money? This is not the old west, Rita. They can track these things now. We can't go around robbing banks. What would we do? Threaten to gum them to death?

RITA
We pack, clean out your account, and split. This tea smells good. What is it?

STEVE
Almond sunset.

RITA takes a tiny sip.

RITA
Tastes a little bitter.

STEVE
Want some more honey?

RITA
(suspiciously)
Yes. Wait. You're not drinking yours.

STEVE
Too hot.

RITA
(switching cups)
I'll drink yours.

STEVE
Ok.

Switches cups. Takes a sip.

RITA
Drink mine!

STEVE
Still too hot.

RITA
You put something in here, didn't you?

STEVE
Maybe I did, maybe I didn't. Point is, we'll never be able to trust each other again, will we?

He sits there, staring at her. Then he moves the tea cups around like three-card monte. He then takes a sip out of one cup.

STEVE
The silence of sin makes me a coward among men. To Maude. Delicious.

RITA
You did it. You really did it. Oh my God!

RITA rushes to the sink and starts gulping water and trying to throw up. She looks in the cupboard, and finds a small vial.

RITA
Potassium arsenate?

STEVE just sits there.

RITA
How much did you use? A teaspoon is already too much.

STEVE
There really was only one way out of this. How are you feeling? I'm feeling a little light-headed myself.

RITA
You bastard! Tit for tat, huh? An eye for an eye? I am getting out of here. I should have killed you when I had the chance, you good for nothing, philandering slug!

RITA runs towards the back door, but is stopped by DETECTIVE BAILEY.

DETECTIVE
I wouldn't rush off quite yet, Ms. Lowenthal.

RITA
You gotta get me to the hospital right away. The tea. He poisoned the tea to get back at me for killing Maude.

STEVE
I did nothing of the sort.

STEVE drinks the tea.

STEVE
My wife has quite the suspicious nature. But feel free to take it with you, Detective. Nothing stronger in there than organic honey.

RITA
You tricked me. You two-timing rat fink!

STEVE
I didn't trick you. I merely stopped you.

DETECTIVE
I am afraid I have to ask you to come with me, ma'am. You have the right to remain silent. Anything you say can and will be used against you in a court of law. You have the right to an attorney. If you cannot afford an attorney, one will be provided for you. I won't place the handcuffs on you. I expect that you will come quietly.

RITA
It was an accident. An unfortunate accident. I was trying to kill that lousy, no good, blood sucking louse of a husband!

STEVE
The truth shall set you free, Rita, but in this case...

DETECTIVE
We have a car waiting outside, Ma'am. It's time to go.

RITA
I went to school with Judge Steinlauf. He's going to see right through this. He always loved me.

DETECTIVE
Judge Steinlauf died in '97. But I am sure you will get a very fair trial. I am sorry, very sorry for everything, Mr. Lowenthal.

STEVE
Me too, officer.

RITA
Detective!

RITA smiles at the detective.

RITA
Did I ever tell you? I was in the Ziegfeld Follies of 1957 at the Winter Garden Theater? I was a contortionist. I've gotten out of tighter spots than this. You'll be seeing me, Steve.

STEVE
Good luck, Rita.

DETECTIVE
By the way, Mr. Lowenthal, we have a little gift for you from the hospital.

MAUDE wheels in through the back door.

STEVE
Maude! How is this possible?

MAUDE
I am so sorry, Steve. We had to do it this way. I knew it wasn't you.

RITA
What? You're alive? What is this, an episode of Ironside? Let go of me, Lt. Columbo. No murder, no crime, right?

STEVE
Maude? What happened?

MAUDE
Is it ok, now?

DETECTIVE nods.

MAUDE
I did eat one of those candies. An orange orange. You were right.
(to RITA)

MAUDE (cont.)
They really are awful, my dear. You definitely should stop making them. I got sick almost immediately. Horrible cramping, headache, sweating, vomiting. It wasn't a pretty sight. The nurses at Brookfield were pretty concerned. Tuesday is pot roast night, after all. It could have been Ebola! I was rushed into the ER, and had my stomach pumped. The marzipan had barely been digested thank goodness but there were traces of–

STEVE
Arsenic trioxide.

MAUDE
I knew immediately who these were meant for, but the police needed to make sure. I hated to deceive you, darling. It must have been awful for you. And Rita, I forgive you. I don't know what I would have done in your position.

STEVE
It wouldn't have been this.

MAUDE
No. But imagining a life without you must have sent her over the edge.

RITA
So, FDR here is willing to forgive and forget. What do we do now, Detective?

DETECTIVE
Are you willing to drop the charges, Ms. Elliot?

MAUDE
Hell no!! Do not confuse my kindness for weakness. I have a tendency to always take the high road, but since she took the low one, I think she should spend some time in the tombs.
(to STEVE)
That is what they call it, right?

MAUDE (cont.)
(to RITA)
Orange is not your color, dear, but I am sure you'll make it work for you.

DETECTIVE
You are under arrest for the attempted murder of Maude Elliot and Steve Lowenthal. You have the right to remain silent.

RITA
Oh, don't bother. I've heard it before. You were in on this together the whole time, weren't you? You two-bit snake in the grass.

RITA breaks away, runs to MAUDE's wheelchair and starts kicking it.

RITA
I hate you! Fuck you, you Stephen Hawking bitch!! I'll take my chances with the law. You'll never live long enough to testify against me! I have friends in low places. Watch your backs! Both of you! This is not over. Not by a long shot. And you–
(to STEVE)
I wouldn't live another day with you if you were dipped in gold!
(to DETECTIVE)
I suppose you're feeling pretty good about yourself.

DETECTIVE
Not particularly. All I did was restore order.

STEVE
Maybe she can plead mental incompetence. I hear some psychiatric facilities have folk dancing.

The DETECTIVE leads RITA outside.

RITA
Screw you and your crippled cyclops concubine! I'm as sane as you! I'll be back to dance on your graves! You'll get yours... I'll tell! I'll tell on your whole family, you swindling swine!

DETECTIVE exits with RITA. RITA continues screaming and spewing insults. STEVE closes the door, crosses to a couch or chair, and collapses with despair. MAUDE wheels up beside him and holds his hand.

There is a long pause.

STEVE
The silence.

MAUDE
I know. Unsettling, isn't it?

STEVE
No, it's wonderful. The absence of sound. I haven't heard it in years.

MAUDE
Should I go?

STEVE
No. It's marvelous to have someone to share the silence with.

MAUDE
What did she mean about your family?

STEVE
My son made a mistake years ago. Misappropriated some funds. It's all behind us now. I didn't discuss finances with her. She would have been furious that I spent my retirement money on anything that didn't involve her.

MAUDE
She could get off, you know. She's a very crafty woman.

STEVE
Highly unlikely. But if she does, we will be long gone. I have always wanted to see Iceland. Looked it up in the guide book. Best thing – virtually no murders ever!

MAUDE
Should I start looking up how to make muffins from whale blubber?

STEVE
We get you well first. We have time.

MAUDE
Not so much. In dog years, I have been dead for half a century.

STEVE kisses her tenderly.

STEVE
We have all the time we need. Let's just sit a moment.
(after a pause)
Scrabble?

MAUDE
I have to tell you. I absolutely HATE Scrabble! But as soon as I am on my feet, I'd be up for a game of Naked Twister.

STEVE
You are my kind of woman.

Lights slowly fade to black, as they hold hands, and look off into the distance, smiling.

END OF PLAY

"Death's very laughable.
Such a cunning little mystery, all done with mirrors."

- PRIVATE LIVES, Noël Coward

DECEPTION

DECEPTION

Bambi Everson

EVERSON
COLEMAN

NEW YORK

AUTHOR'S NOTE

I have always been a fan of those quickie film noirs cranked out by lesser studios. TOO LATE FOR TEARS with Lizbeth Scott, DETOUR with Ann Savage. Low budgets but great actors, atmosphere, locations, and of course, your average person caught in a web of deceit that has them circling the drain. These are my comfort foods and during lockdown, I was plenty hungry.

It was difficult for me to write at all when Covid struck, and I was not a fan of the Zoom world that was foisted upon us. One of my great joys becoming a playwright late in life was the personal connections I made with wonderful actors who breathed life into my words. I decided to write a short film noir for the actors I missed and wanted to see again, even in the ether of Zoomland.

But where to start? In my playwriting class, we were given an exercise called, "What if?" where we explored alternative plot lines, and it really resonated with me. I often read movie log lines – short 1 to 2 sentences to entice a viewer – as a prompt for myself. I came across one that said, "A one night stand leads to unfortunate consequences." I thought, "That speaks to me," and started writing with a few favorite actors in mind.

I have worked with the wonderful Emily Strong a few times, and always found that she came up with a delivery I had never thought of. I love working with her, so I wrote in a small part for myself – a) to save money (I work cheap), and b) to be with actors I loved, if only in a small Zoom box.

I am a huge fan of Anthony T. Goss. Anthony has been in several of my plays, and is so good that the feedback has always been MORE ANTHONY. He has great instincts and timing, and makes me laugh at things I didn't think were jokes.

Then there is the sublime Jeremy Lister, who I was very lucky to nab because he is always doing something. Our connection was something akin to Lana Turner being discovered in Schwab's drug store. I saw him late at night on the A train, deftly dealing with a religious zealot.

I commented on his compassion, and asked if he was a therapist. "Nope, I'm an actor," he lamented, which of course was much more exciting to me. We exchanged information, and Jeremy did a reading of a short play of mine in my writers' group. He instantly became part of my beloved core of actors, which I am so grateful for.

I dashed DECEPTION out quickly, without too much research into police procedurals, and learned after the fact that LAW AND ORDER takes liberties, too, so should not be my only form of investigative studies. I attempted to fix some inconsistencies, but I wanted to keep DECEPTION a four-person play, so some remain for "dramatic license." My favorite films have blunders as well, but I love them all the same.

This was a necessary play to write to put a little gas in the empty tank that COVID left me with.

Bambi Everson
New York City, April 2022

PRODUCTION HISTORY

Reading – via Zoom, 2020
With Emily Strong, Jeremy Lister*, Bambi Everson* and Anthony T. Goss

Emily Strong, Jeremy Lister (top l to r), Anthony T. Goss (bottom)*

Emily Strong, Jeremy Lister (top l to r), Bambi Everson* (bottom)*

* appearing with permission of Actors' Equity Association.

DECEPTION
By Bambi Everson
One act, approximately 55 minutes

CHARACTERS:

MADDIE (Female, age/race flexible): Guarded, hopeful, a film geek to the Nth degree.
RICHARD (Male, age/race flexible): Charming, possibly a liar. If so, a good one.
JAN (Female, but age/race flexible, but older than Richard): Hard working and enthusiastic HR employee. Hidden secrets. Hides her unhappiness well.
OFFICER (Male, age/race flexible): New to the job. Careful and sensitive. Can double as MAN in last scene.

PLACE: New York City.
TIME: The present.

SYNOPSIS: A brief encounter in a bar leads to a complicated entanglement. Dishonesty and lying are rampant, but who is doing what?

SCENE 1

MADDIE sits at a bar stool in Kenny's bar. She has a book. She is drinking a glass of water. RICHARD enters. He has a phone in his hand, which he hangs up as he enters.

RICHARD
Wow!! Did you see that?

MADDIE looks up.

MADDIE
See what?

RICHARD
A guy just leapt off the scaffolding.

MADDIE
Oh, my God!

RICHARD
No, I mean, he flew like Superman. Landed on a guy that was stealing a lady's purse. I heard her scream, and saw this dude running down the street, and the next second– *wham!* The dude straddled the guy. Like a hawk.

MADDIE
Was he hurt?

RICHARD
Who?

MADDIE
Anyone.

RICHARD
That's the thing. It was like a ballet. The man landed perfectly. Took the purse right out of the dude's hand. I thought it had to be a movie.

MADDIE
Probably was. They are always shooting something in this neighborhood.

RICHARD
Nope. I looked. A legit New York moment. It was exhilarating.

MADDIE
That's a nice story. I hope you're not making it up.

RICHARD
I'm not. If you knew me, you'd know I don't have the imagination to make stuff like that up.

MADDIE
I don't know you.

RICHARD
Right.

MADDIE turns away, and picks up her book again. RICHARD moves down the bar. He orders a drink from the unseen bartender. A police siren is heard. RICHARD turns to MADDIE, as if to say, "See?" MADDIE nods, and goes back to her book.

RICHARD
Can I buy you a drink?

MADDIE
I don't drink.

RICHARD
You know this is a bar, right?

MADDIE
Cheese fries.

RICHARD
Excuse me?

MADDIE
I'm just here for the cheese fries. Best in the neighborhood.

RICHARD
Ah. Can I buy you some cheese fries?

MADDIE
Waiting on them. Not interested.

RICHARD
Ok.

RICHARD walks away. MADDIE sits and waits for her cheese fries. They arrive, and she eats them. She looks at RICHARD, He is having a drink and not looking at her. MADDIE looks away. Continues eating. After a beat or three...

MADDIE
Thank you.

RICHARD
For what?

MADDIE
Respecting my boundaries.

RICHARD
No means no. I wasn't raised by wolves.

MADDIE
Yeah, but some guys are real dicks, ya know?

RICHARD
I'm a dick.

MADDIE
Figures.

RICHARD
I'm Richard.

MADDIE
Ah.

RICHARD
I never understood how people get Dick from Richard.

MADDIE
Interested? 'Cause I just happen to know...

RICHARD
(indicating moving closer)
Yeah... May I?

MADDIE nods and RICHARD slides into the next stool.

RICHARD
Hit me.

MADDIE
Goes back to the middle ages when everybody had to write things by hand. So people shortened them. Richard became Rich or Rick. People back then liked rhyming nicknames. Rick, Dick... Get it?

RICHARD
Got it.

MADDIE
Dick became a euphemism for… um, you know… from Chaucer, I think. Canterbury Tales. The verb "dighte" means copulation.

RICHARD
Ah! Taking a little break from the Google tonight?

MADDIE
English teacher. History buff.

RICHARD
Cool. What grade?

MADDIE
Not teaching anymore. Long story. But I'm starting a new job tomorrow, so I am here celebrating.

RICHARD
With cheese fries? Not much of a celebration.

MADDIE
I don't have much of a paycheck. Yet.

RICHARD
Since you don't drink, could I at least buy you a dessert? A smoothie? Vegan ice cream? As a thank you for the edifying word origin?

MADDIE
I am not in the habit of picking up strange men in bars.

RICHARD
Neither am I. You don't seem particularly strange. I just saw something outside that blew my mind. I feel like anything is possible. Now I want to pay it forward. I want to do something for somebody else.

MADDIE
You could tip the bartender.

RICHARD
I will.

RICHARD puts five dollars on the counter, and pushes it over to where he was sitting. He checks to see if she noticed. Silence. MADDIE finishes, or has finished, her cheese fries. She drinks her water.

RICHARD
Don't you find this bar a little depressing? It's so dark.

MADDIE
I like dark.

RICHARD
Ah. A woman of mystery.

MADDIE
Not really. Food is cheap. I know the bartender. What is that concoction you are drinking anyway?

RICHARD
Interested? I'll order you one– Right, you don't drink.

MADDIE
Not that strange stuff. Wine with my spaghetti, but I usually fall off my chair after one glass.

RICHARD
This baby is a Paradise Mule.

MADDIE
Who comes up with these ridiculous names?

RICHARD
You are the history expert. This has Absolut lime vodka, pineapple, ginger beer, and Blue Butterfly Blossom. Boosts the immune system.

MADDIE
That is some hippy dippy drink, for sure.

RICHARD
Sure you don't want a sip? You can use your own straw. Obviously, it's safe. No drugs...

MADDIE
Why would you even say that? And no, I think I'll pass.

RICHARD
I just wanted you to feel comfortable with me. I watch a lot of "Law and Order SVU." I'm not a creep. Not charming enough to be a predator.

MADDIE
That's exactly what a predator would say.

RICHARD
I'm sorry. I'm blowing this badly. I'll leave you alone.

RICHARD slides back to his seat and slips a $20 bill to the unseen bartender and leaves. MADDIE takes a moment, sighs, drops some money on the table, gathers herself and leaves the bar.

LIGHTS CHANGE, SCENE CONTINUES

We are now on the street. RICHARD is standing in front of the bar.

RICHARD
Have a nice night.

MADDIE
Oh no! You weren't seriously waiting out here for me, were you? 'Cause that would be creepy.

RICHARD
Nope. Just waiting for my Lyft.

RICHARD shows MADDIE his cell phone.

RICHARD
Five minutes away.

MADDIE
Oh, God. I'm sorry. I have literally no people skills, in case you didn't notice.

RICHARD
I wasn't going to say anything.

MADDIE
It's not funny.

RICHARD
Not laughing.

MADDIE
I'm starting a new job tomorrow. I have one chance to show people I'm not the weird girl. One shot to fake I am somebody else. Somebody competent. What's the use? I'll probably get fired. I'm not a team player. I'm just more comfortable in my own little corner, not distracted by office parties, and baby showers, or donuts in the staff lounge.

RICHARD
You don't like donuts? That is weird.

MADDIE
I love donuts. I just grab and run. Eating isn't a social event for me. It's private. Like peeing or masturbating... Fuck. My filter just sprung a leak. Have a nice life.

MADDIE starts walking away.

RICHARD
Wanna lift? My ride should be here in...
(checks his phone)
Still 5 minutes. Crap. Maybe I should just start walking, too.

MADDIE
Why would I get into a car with you?

RICHARD
1. It's Lyft. There will probably be other people in the car. 2. We're not exactly strangers anymore. 3. I know you're starting a new job, you only drink wine with spaghetti, and that you hate social events. Whenever I meet an intriguing person, I always convince them to divulge their secrets.

MADDIE
Mine aren't all that interesting.

RICHARD
Maybe that changes tonight. Tomorrow, you get to be a whole new you. Why not practice now? When was the last time you attempted something out of the ordinary?

MADDIE
Been a while. You are really good at retaining information.

RICHARD
Only when I'm interested.

MADDIE
In high school, I kissed a boy at a party just because he understood my obscure film reference. I'm a film nerd.

RICHARD
Ah!

MADDIE
I didn't even know his name. He asked me if I was "part of this circus" and I said, "No, but I have an aunt with an elephant act."

RICHARD shrugs. He has no clue.

MADDIE
He said if I was going to quote Roland Young, he would quote Franklin Pangborn. So, I kissed him. Hard.

RICHARD
I wouldn't have gotten kissed that night. But I would have wanted to.

MADDIE looks at him for a moment, then impulsively kisses him. Then pulls back, shocked at her behavior.

MADDIE
Oh, my God! I am so sorry. This is not like me at all.

RICHARD
Maybe it is you. Maybe it's the new you.

Looks at cell phone.

RICHARD
Two minutes away.

MADDIE
Hold on.

She pulls out her phone.

MADDIE
I need a picture of us. To commemorate the start of the new me. Or if you turn out to be a serial killer, I got you.

RICHARD
Get my best side.

MADDIE takes a few pictures.

RICHARD
You are very thorough. It just occurred to me. I don't even know your name.

MADDIE
That's right, you don't. It's... Carol... Carol... Brady.

RICHARD
Oh, so we are going to play that game. Alright. I'm...

MADDIE
Richard.

RICHARD
Yup... Richard... Burton. Come on, Carol, your chariot awaits.

There is a honk from a car. They look at each other. He takes her hand, and they walk towards the car.

BLACKOUT

SCENE 2

Next day. MADDIE is being walked around her new job by JAN, the office manager.

JAN
So, this is your area. We try to keep things pretty tidy around here. Mr. Haloren is a bit of a stickler. You can put up a picture of your pet, or your kid, of course, just... you know, don't plaster the sides with them. The last woman used her dog pictures as camouflage, so we couldn't see she was sleeping, or watching Netflix. Your workload is sent to your office email daily. Surveys, audio transcriptions, Honestly, it's pretty boring. You can keep your phone on, in case of emergency, but no inter-office texting, or candy crush, obviously.

MADDIE
Obviously.

JAN
The gender-neutral bathroom is down the hall. Hope you are ok with that.

MADDIE
Of course.

JAN
You'll need a key, which is at my desk, so I'll know if you are in there longer than it takes for your average–

MADDIE
Got it.

JAN
In case you missed this in the manual, you get a half hour for lunch. Most of us eat at our desks but you are welcome to leave the building. The lines around here are crazy, though, so I recommend brown-bagging or ordering in. You get two 15-minute breaks during the day. Some

JAN (cont.)
people string them together for a one-hour lunch, but I really think you'll need a break from screen time, so I recommend taking them and chilling out in the staff lounge which is–

MADDIE
The big room at the end.

JAN
Right. There is a vending machine, but the guy who refills it hasn't been around for months. You didn't hear it from me, but I think he's been arrested. He had bad teeth, and his pupils were pinpoints. But we try to avoid gossip around here. Office relationships are strongly discouraged. But look around, present company excluded, of course. It's pretty slim pickings around here. I knew right away you seemed like a cut above our average research assistant. I'm glad to have you aboard, but can I ask what made you say yes?

MADDIE
Is this a necessary part of my orientation?

JAN
Nope. Just curious. I know you were a teacher. Quikster Analytics is radically different. No kids. Deathly quiet. Isolating.

MADDIE
Sounds good.

JAN
It can be hard if you are a social animal. I go weeks without having a conversation. We have bagel Mondays, but nobody really talks about their weekends. Most of us don't have much of a life. You seem different.

MADDIE
Different good?

JAN
I'm hoping so.

MADDIE
I'll save my sad story for another time.

JAN
A sex scandal?

MADDIE
God, no.

JAN
Stealing school supplies?

MADDIE
Not even toilet paper. I was a Girl Scout.

JAN
No shit! Me too! Troop 3-261. Come on... off the record. Girl Scout's honor.

MADDIE
It's just I was privy to some information about my former employer. An investigator asked us all questions privately, and I told the truth. I'm a really crappy liar.

JAN
Ooh! A sex scandal??

MADDIE
Life must really be dull here around the water cooler.

JAN
You have no idea.

MADDIE
Admissions bribery. The principal got in some hot water. Fired, actually. I guess I was responsible. I left because I felt the hatred from the other teachers. Apparently, I should have protected her.

JAN
You did the right thing. The truth always wins in the end. Shows you have character.

MADDIE
Well, my character got me blackballed from teaching.

JAN
Your story is safe with me.

MADDIE
Are you the person in charge or–

JAN
Mr. Haloren rarely socializes with staff, but he's accessible. A regular Lou Grant. His office is over there. You have a problem; it goes through me first. I'm HR, among other things, and then if it can't be solved in-house, it goes to the boss.

MADDIE
Is he–

JAN
He's great. A peach. Of course, I am paid to say that.

MADDIE
Right.

JAN
I'm one of those people who takes their work home with them. Jan Haloren. Married to the boss.

MADDIE
Oh!

JAN
Way before he started this company. He said he couldn't do it without me, but I think I'm cheap labor. Anyway... Works out. We don't have kids or pets, so the long hours don't bother us. How 'bout you?

MADDIE
I guess I can handle long (ish) hours...

JAN
I meant kids... I know we aren't supposed to ask.

MADDIE
No, I am ridiculously and emphatically unattached.

JAN
Any other questions?

MADDIE
I guess not. Thanks. Should I…

JAN
Oh, right. I should have you go in and meet Mr. Haloren.

JAN goes to her desk and picks up the intercom phone.

JAN
Madeline McKenzie is here. She's up to speed now. She'll be starting with the Edwards account. Do you want...
(to MADDIE)
Go on in. Don't worry, honey. He's gonna love you.

MADDIE thanks JAN and goes to the door.

LIGHTS TRANSITION TO OFFICE. SCENE CONTINUES.

MADDIE
Oh, crap.

RICHARD
Carol Brady! What are the odds?

MADDIE
Richard Burton... Guess I'll be leaving now. I was really hoping my next job would last longer than Rudolph Valentino's first marriage. My karma sucks.

She starts to exit. RICHARD jumps up, closes the door and makes sure no one can hear.

RICHARD
No. No. Don't go! Please...

MADDIE
This is ridiculous.

RICHARD
You can't leave now.

MADDIE
Well, I can't stay. I just met your wife.

RICHARD
Awkward, for sure. But... nothing happened!

MADDIE
We kissed. A lot. I don't consider that nothing, thank you very much.

RICHARD
Oh! I didn't mean it like that. And technically, you kissed me first.

MADDIE
That's your reasoning? I started it?

RICHARD
Of course not. The kissing... was... lovely. A lovely mistake on my part. I take full responsibility.

MADDIE
So, now I am a mistake? I am outta here.

RICHARD
How do I explain it? I suffer from foot-in-mouth disease. I can be a dunderhead, a jerk. But I am not a bad person. Jan does the hiring. She said you were the most qualified applicant to walk through these doors in years. Can we just move on from the fact that we both had momentary lapses in judgment?

MADDIE
Speak for yourself. I didn't have any regrets... Until a few moments ago.

RICHARD
I still want you to work here. You are a very unique and unusual human. I like you.

MADDIE
So... What? I start this job lying? So much for me being whoever I want to be.

RICHARD
You are the kind of person we need around here. Someone with a brain, and a sense of humor, not just Google skills. Besides, if I fired you today, you could claim unfair termination. Jan would find that really strange.

MADDIE
You don't know me. I wouldn't do that. Don't you think it would be harder on you if I stayed? You'd be walking on eggshells, wondering if I'd ever spill the beans about our romantic ride from Kenny's bar.

RICHARD
You would certainly have the upper hand. Hey, can I ask a stupid question?

MADDIE
Why stop now?

RICHARD
Valentino...

MADDIE
Really?

RICHARD
...

MADDIE
Fine. His first marriage ended at the reception. Never consummated.

RICHARD
Were they able to stay friends?

MADDIE
How should I know? It was 1919.

RICHARD
Are we? Able to be friends?

MADDIE
It's going to be weird.

RICHARD
Only if we make it so.

MADDIE
I was really looking forward to this fucking job.

There is a knock at the door and JAN enters.

JAN
Geez, what are you two doing in here? Getting married?
(laughing uncomfortably)

RICHARD
(annoyed)
What is it? Ms. Mackenzie and I were just ironing out a few things.

JAN
Sorry. Benny has an IT issue that is beyond me. Can you take a look? And shouldn't Maddie get started on the Edwards account? You know how he is about meeting deadlines.

RICHARD
Edwards is an ass. It can wait. Throw the account to Ian. He'll be glad for the extra work. I'm putting Ms. McKenzie in charge of stock footage. Apparently, she's quite the history buff.

MADDIE
I'm not sure...

JAN
(to MADDIE)
You got some sins you need to atone for? Come on, Richard, we don't want to lose her. She'll bring some cheerfulness into this joint. God knows, we need that.

RICHARD
I am aware. Ms. McKenzie? It's up to you. I'm fine either way. Because of your level of proficiency in this area, we can offer you an extra $100 a week, and commissions on any project that you have specifically spearheaded.

JAN
Sounds like bribery to me. Just kidding! Take it! Nobody else around here wants, or is even capable of doing it. I'll show you the ropes.

MADDIE
Maybe it's not... (the right fit)

JAN
For an extra $100 a week, I'd do it myself, if I could, but I can't. Are we still negotiating? How about we throw in free snacks from the vending machine? I had a key copied in case of a nuclear disaster.

MADDIE
I guess...
(looks at RICHARD)
Are you sure?

RICHARD
Never surer.

MADDIE
Ok. Then.

JAN
Stale Doritos for the win!

RICHARD
Welcome to Quickster Analytics.

JAN
Thank goodness that's settled, then. We have about a thousand hours of old celebrities we can't identify, and hundreds of hours of old commercials. The past keeps increasing so you could easily get lost in there.

MADDIE
"The past is a ghost, the future a dream, and all we ever have is now."

RICHARD
Cool quote. Who said that? Nietzsche?

MADDIE
Bill Cosby. Weird, huh?

RICHARD
Jan, lunch is on me today. Everyone can take a full hour. No lost time. To welcome our new employee. Send a memo. Conference room, 12:30. We'll order from Capital Diner. Get some veggie, and turkey burgers, a few salads, some desserts and uh... four orders of cheese fries.

JAN
Cheese fries? Eww! Heart attack on a plate. Who is going to eat those?

MADDIE and RICHARD exchange a glance.

BLACKOUT

SCENE 3

A couple of weeks later. MADDIE is at her desk. JAN approaches.

JAN
That was amazing.

MADDIE
Thanks.

JAN
Where do you find this stuff?

MADDIE
My dad was a film historian. There's some great public domain stuff out there that no one has heard of, except us weird film geeks.

JAN
Well, the client loved the insurance campaign. Richard is talking about a bonus on top of your commission.

MADDIE
That's unexpected.

JAN
When's your next break?

MADDIE
Didn't take one yet. I usually don't need it so...

JAN
Can we talk?

MADDIE
Sure.

JAN
Privately?

MADDIE
Sure. Here or...

JAN looks around, seeing there is no one around, pulls a chair over to MADDIE's work area.

JAN
Here's good. I'm sure you know by now that I like you.

MADDIE
Thank you?

JAN
I don't have any friends here. Or anywhere, really.

MADDIE
Oh, I'm sure that's not–

JAN
Oh, it is. I'm the boss' wife. Nobody trusts me. Nobody tells me anything.

MADDIE
What do you need to know? We all have pretty boring lives, as far as I can tell.

JAN
Nobody eats with me at lunch. They see me in the conference room, and they just turn on their heels and leave. You'd think cozying up to me would be a good thing. But no...

MADDIE
I'll talk to them if you want... but most people choose this type of work because they lack social skills. I wouldn't take it personally. Besides, you were pretty clear about office relationships in the orientation.

JAN
Relationships. Not fraternizing. I don't need to be invited to anyone's wedding... Ok, wedding would be a stretch, considering, but no one even shows me a picture of their new cat. No one ever asks about my weekend.

MADDIE
How was your weekend?

JAN
Awful. Thanks for asking.

MADDIE
I'm sorry.

JAN
Don't you want to know why?

MADDIE
Of course. Do you want some chocolate? I keep a secret stash here.

JAN
Dark?

MADDIE
Is there any other?

MADDIE opens a drawer and takes out a bar of Lindt dark chocolate. She breaks off a few squares and hands it to JAN, who hungrily accepts and wolfs it down.

JAN
Oh, my God! So good. Richard doesn't allow me to eat chocolate.

MADDIE
Doesn't allow?

JAN
I just mean... He doesn't want it in the house. For my own good, I suppose.

MADDIE
I don't approve of people denying themselves things they love, unless, of course, it's going to kill you. That's not the case, is it?

JAN
I'm not a diabetic, or a dog. I can eat chocolate. I can eat anything. I just don't. Richard...

MADDIE
Ah, we're back to Richard again.

JAN
He's always been a bit controlling, you know. What's mine is his, and what's his is his. It wasn't an issue at first. I liked being married. I wasn't sure it was even in the cards for me. I'm older than Richard. You probably guessed. 16 years. It was cool when he was 19, and I could buy alcohol for him... but now, the gap gets larger every year.

MADDIE
It's probably a really bad idea for me to get into the middle of anything personal between you two. Maybe therapy? A good counselor? I could make some inquiries.

JAN
He would never. He's pulling away, and I'm pretty sure he's up to something. On Sunday, he left a journal entry up on his computer, like he wanted me to see it. He doesn't make mistakes like that. It was

JAN (cont.)
purposeful. Something about another woman. Carol somebody... I've always suspected there were others. Son of a bitch...

MADDIE
That sounds pretty crappy to me, if it's true.

JAN
Oh, it's true. Outside of these walls, Richard is pretty damn charming. Women literally throw themselves at him. You don't see that side of him.

MADDIE
No. I don't.

JAN
Been going on for some time. Once we were in the supermarket, and a young woman threw an egg at him. Another time, he was picking up dry cleaning, and I was waiting outside, and a woman called him by name, and then spit in his general direction. He pretended these women were crazy, but I'm not an idiot.

MADDIE
I'm so sorry.

JAN
I could leave him. I probably should. The company is in my name, you know. It's my money behind it. If he doesn't straighten up and fly right, I could close down this whole operation. Strike out on my own. I'm seriously thinking about it. I could open a perfume factory in France, or a cat cafe in Weehawken. What do you think?

MADDIE
I think cat cafes are awesome, and life is short. No one should wake up every morning with regrets. If you are unhappy, I would encourage you to leave. But I don't really know your situation, and to be frank... I don't think I am the one you should be talking to. Don't you have a best friend? A sister?

JAN
I haven't spoken to my family in years. I eloped with Richard rather spontaneously. We honeymooned in Europe on my dime. Richard didn't even have a job then. He played chess in the park for money.

MADDIE
Was he good?

JAN
Really good. He always thought three moves ahead. But he couldn't make a go of it, professionally. He talked me into starting this company. That's my life. Here, and home, and lately, I am home alone more often than not. He calls me all the time on our landline, he says just to hear my voice, but I know it's just to make sure I'm there. He hears my voice all damn day, every day.

MADDIE
Seems to me, you need some time to work things out. Why don't you take the day and do something for yourself? I'll cover for you. I'll say your lunch didn't sit right, and you needed to go.

JAN
He has a GPS on my phone.

MADDIE
Really? Ok. Leave it with me. I'll say you left in a hurry and forgot it. I'll give it to Mr... to Richard. Email me if you get nervous.

JAN
He tracks my emails.

MADDIE
Jesus, Jan– I would never put up with that. Just take the day. Experience a little freedom.

JAN
Ha! What's that?

MADDIE
Get away from these four walls, and be yourself for a while.

JAN
Good advice. I'm getting a trashy novel, and a keratin treatment for my hair. Richard always thought that was an extravagance.

MADDIE
That's your idea of freedom? Whatever. I am not one to judge. Here.

MADDIE reaches into her drawer and pulls out a $100 bill.

JAN
No. What's this for?

MADDIE
In case he checks your credit card transactions. Frankly, I would spend some of the day opening up your own account. It's your money. This is not the 1950s anymore. Take back your control.

JAN
You're right. Hair first. Bank second. You're a doll. And thanks. It feels good to have a real friend at last. I'll pay you back tomorrow.

JAN takes the money, hands over her cell phone and starts to leave.

MADDIE
(sotto voce)
JAN... Your purse!

JAN grabs her purse, feigns being sick and runs out. MADDIE quietly returns JAN's cell phone to her desk. No one has noticed anything. Visibly shaken, she breathes deeply, eats chocolate and resumes typing.

BLACKOUT or LIGHT SHIFT INDICATES PASSAGE OF TIME

SCENE 4

A few hours later. JAN's office phone rings. MADDIE freezes. She looks around to see if anyone else will pick it up. No one does. She walks over and picks up the phone.

MADDIE
Jan Haloren's desk. No, Mr. Haloren, this is Maddie. Jan had to leave. She said she was feeling sick. Said the chicken salad was probably off.
(Pause)
Ok.

MADDIE hangs up the phone and returns to her desk. A moment later, JAN's cell phone rings and rings. Then, the office phone rings again. MADDIE answers it.

MADDIE
Jan Haloren's desk... Yes. Yes, it was. I'm not sure. Yes. It's here. Alright.

MADDIE takes the phone and brings it into RICHARD's office, knocking first. LIGHTS change to interior of RICHARD's office.

MADDIE
She left in a bit of a hurry. She took her purse, but must have forgotten the phone.

RICHARD
Jan hasn't been sick a day in her life. She has the constitution of a vulture.

MADDIE
She did look a bit green when she left. I hope she feels better soon.

RICHARD
She likes you.

MADDIE
I like her, too.

RICHARD
That's a bit of a problem.

MADDIE
How so?

RICHARD
I like you, too.

MADDIE
I'm not–

RICHARD
I haven't stopped thinking about you since that night.

MADDIE
That was another me. Another time.

RICHARD
Can you honestly say you haven't felt the energy between us?

MADDIE
Yes. I can honestly say that. I have done many things that I am not proud of, but I am not, never have been, a home-wrecker and this... this right here is really inappropriate.

RICHARD
Has she confided in you?

MADDIE
No. Your personal life is none of my business.

RICHARD
I think she knows.

MADDIE
Not from me.

RICHARD
Our marriage was like a ski jump. We just leapt off into the void. Reckless. You behave like that when you're young. Jan and I are welded together like a pipe, but going in two different directions. A boring dinner, with no dessert. Then, you happened. You were the ice cream sundae I'd been missing all these years.

MADDIE
Stop. I am nobody's ice cream. Figure out your life. This is an impossible situation. I shouldn't have agreed to it in the first place.

RICHARD
Maybe deep down inside, you wanted this?

MADDIE
No.

RICHARD
Look, we both did a great job of being professional. Admit it. It's been hard. But I caught them – the glances, the electricity that occurred when our hands accidentally brushed. Couldn't you sense my hunger? Just standing next to you in the elevator, I have to hold my breath, so I don't blurt out how much I want you. Your brain is an aphrodisiac to me. That geeky movie-speak... it's so goddamned sexy. You are quirky and imaginative and remarkable, and I have been silently but steadfastly falling for you. I think together we could be a magical combination, Lucy and Desi... Sorry... I don't have your skills for movie references, but you get my drift. Creative partners at work – and in life...

MADDIE
My God! You really are an asshole. So was Desi Arnaz. That's a shit analogy! I wanted the job. The job only. And the kicker is, I'm really good at it. If I told HR my side of the story, your sorry ass would be fired. Frankly, that is very tempting.

RICHARD
Jan is HR.

MADDIE
I fucking know that! I also know she'd feel very betrayed by me. So, thanks for that. I like her. I really do. She's caught on to your extracurricular activities, and now I feel complicit, and let me tell you, that's a really crappy feeling. Why Jan hasn't left you is beyond me, but that's between you two. I can't do this. I quit. I'll come back tomorrow, clean out my desk, and hand the files over to Jan. I'll make it as smooth a transition as possible.

RICHARD
I don't know what Jan has told you, but I want to make one thing clear. Jan plays the victim really well, but she got exactly what she wanted in this marriage. Jan's family gave her money, but nothing else, no self-worth, no love. I came along and gave her that. She thought she'd won the husband lottery. I'm not gonna lie. Her money talked. All my money ever said was, "See ya." I'm not an evil guy. Just floundering. My love faded. That's a tragedy, not a crime. That night in the bar, we were just two people in the moment. It was a singular, hedonistic impulse. One we would have remembered with fondness. You walking in here the next day... that was fate. Fate can change your life in an instant.

MADDIE
It sure was one heck of a coincidence.

RICHARD
Maddie, please... For once, let's not be sensible.

MADDIE falters for a moment. She nearly gives in.

MADDIE
No. I can't.

RICHARD
I did the right thing. I chose not to act on my feelings. But they wouldn't go away. A man can only stand so much. I think it's wrong to avoid what was clearly destiny. Let me ask you a question. If I wasn't married...

MADDIE
But you are, Richard. I am not going to delve into hypotheticals with you. This is not some Noel Coward play. I can't do this. Fuck you. Fuck you for putting me in this position.

MADDIE storms out of the office, grabs her purse and exits. RICHARD comes out of his office and looks around.

RICHARD
Anyone else have issues with me today? Back to work, then. We have a deadline. If anyone hears from my wife, let me know.

RICHARD stomps back into his office as the lights dim.

BLACKOUT

SCENE 5

The next day. MADDIE enters the office. She looks around. No one is there. She checks her watch. Goes to look in the conference room. No one.

MADDIE
Hello? Anyone here?

MADDIE walks to her desk and opens a drawer. OFFICER ANDREWS enters. He is anxious.

OFFICER
Hold it right there, Lady! Don't move! Police officer! Hands where I can see them!

MADDIE screams!

MADDIE
My hands are here! Look! Don't shoot!

OFFICER
Mr. Haloren... Do you know this woman?

RICHARD enters.

RICHARD
My God! Maddie. What are you doing here?

MADDIE
Cleaning out my desk. Jesus Christ. Can I put my hands down now?

RICHARD
(to OFFICER)
It's fine. She's fine.

OFFICER
(putting away gun)
Ok. Can't be too careful these days.

RICHARD
Didn't you get my email? I sent it to everyone in the office.

MADDIE
Well, I don't technically work here anymore, so I didn't check. What's going on? Did you get robbed?

RICHARD
Jan is dead.

MADDIE
What?? What do you mean, dead?

RICHARD
Dead. As in – the fucking morgue. As in – awaiting an autopsy.

MADDIE
Oh, no!! What happened?

RICHARD
I found her last night. It's a nightmare. I haven't slept yet. Officer Andrews escorted me back here. I'm closing up shop for the time being, and the cops are checking everything, as they do. I can't be home. Cops are everywhere. I can still feel her blood on me.

MADDIE
I don't understand.

OFFICER
It looks like it was a terrible accident, Miss...

MADDIE
Mckenzie. Ms.

OFFICER
Ms. Mckenzie. Officer Andrews. Nice to meet you. Sorry for the circumstances. And the gun... People don't take too kindly to police officers these days.

MADDIE
Can you understand why??

OFFICER
I get it. Sorry again. Are you ok with answering a few questions?

RICHARD
Don't you need a... partner or something?

OFFICER
...Yeah. Lemme call my supervisor. Excuse me.

OFFICER goes off to the side to make a call, while still watching MADDIE and RICHARD. They are silent for a moment, watching the OFFICER watch them.

MADDIE
I am stunned. Completely gutted. Jan was.... I was so fond of her. Are you ok?

RICHARD
Of course, I am not ok! But thanks for asking.

OFFICER returns.

OFFICER
Ok. My supervisor says it's fine to ask some informal questions. We could take you down to the station, but we have to finish up here, and my partner is still at the house with the forensic team, so...

MADDIE
It's ok. Anything to help. I can't believe it. She was fine yesterday.

OFFICER
Mr. Haloren said she left here yesterday, sick.

MADDIE
Well, yes and no.

RICHARD
What do you mean, "No?" You are the one who told me she was green, and heading home.

MADDIE
It's complicated.

OFFICER
How so?

RICHARD
Maddie, if it's about my wife, I wanna know. I need to know. I came home last night, and found her in the tub. She must have slipped reaching for something. The towel rack was pulled down. There was blood in the water. She must have hit her head on the spigot. I pulled her out and performed CPR, but it was too late. I called 911. I saw them take my wife out of my house in a body bag! I want to know how this could have happened.

MADDIE
It's too horrible. Poor Jan.

OFFICER
Ms. McKenzie, apparently you were the last one to speak with her yesterday. You said she was ill. Was she heading to the doctor?

MADDIE
She wasn't really "sick" sick. She just needed a little time.

RICHARD
What are you saying? You said it was the chicken salad.

MADDIE
Officer, I said that. I covered for Jan. She just... needed a break.

OFFICER
A break from what?

RICHARD
She could have taken a break anytime she wanted to. She owned the company–

OFFICER
Mr. Haloren, please! Ms. MacKenzie, did Mrs. Haloren tell you where she was headed?

MADDIE
Just away. She wanted to think things through.

OFFICER
What kind of things?

RICHARD
Hold up. This is where things get weird, Officer. I'm not doing myself any favors telling you this, but ...there was trouble between Jan and me. Involving another woman. Jan was pretty angry at me, rightly so. She was depressed. Sometimes she drank at night. Not that much, never missed a day of work. But we weren't really speaking outside of the office, and I tended to stay away from home. But this? I wouldn't wish that sight on my worst enemy. I'll never get that picture out of my head. There was so much blood! How can I ever set foot in there again? In that bathroom where she–

OFFICER
Yes. A very unpleasant discovery, for sure. Things always get sticky when there is a third party involved. Do you think your wife might have been despondent over the other woman? That the knowledge of your affair might have prompted her to drink a little heavier than usual last night? Might she have supplemented her imbibing with some pills?

RICHARD
It's possible. I'm not sure. She took Ambien to sleep, and Celexa or maybe Paxil during the day. They'd be in the medicine cabinet.

OFFICER
Well, the autopsy will sort all that out.

MADDIE
No.

OFFICER
No, what?

MADDIE
No, it's not possible that she deliberately tried to die by suicide.

OFFICER
What makes you think that?

MADDIE
What woman would go to the hairdresser if she was just going to kill herself in the bathtub?

OFFICER
You'd be surprised how many people decide to leave a beautiful corpse behind.

RICHARD
There was nothing beautiful about the way I found her. I resent that, Officer.

OFFICER
I understand how difficult this is, but we need to explore every angle while we wait on the autopsy. Mr. Haloren. I suggest you give me the name of the woman in question. Just so I can verify whereabouts. You understand. We are not accusing anyone of anything. Just for clarity's sake.

RICHARD
It wasn't like that. It was an emotional affair. Are you married, Officer?

OFFICER
Just to my job, Mr. Haloren. I am in the honeymoon phase.

RICHARD
Just my luck to get a rookie.

OFFICER
I assure you; you are in capable and determined hands. Maybe I go too far sometimes, but that's where you find the truth. I want to sort this all out as swiftly as possible, so we can all rest easy. No pun intended, Mr. Haloren. Now, about this "emotional affair." Your wife knew?

RICHARD
These kinds of hiccups happen in a marriage from time to time. You think you are in love with someone, but it's a fantasy. And if it's one sided, it will really play with you, mentally. I am ashamed to admit that during this period of instability, I wasn't very kind to Jan. I was torn. Jan was upset. Obviously, she confided in Maddie, which is ironic.

OFFICER
How so?

MADDIE
Don't go there. I was her friend. Maybe her only friend. Richard kept her on a short leash.

OFFICER
Just exactly what was your relationship with Mr. Haloren, Ms. McKenzie?

MADDIE
None. There was no relationship. Contrary to what Richard – Mr. Haloren – might be implying. We had a moment before I started working here.

OFFICER
What do you mean by "a moment?"

MADDIE
We met in a bar. It was one of those crazy coincidences. I don't believe in destiny. I didn't want to work here after... but I needed to work. Unlike some people in this room, I am not financially supported by someone else. We agreed to put our "moment" behind us. I did. I did not deliberately become friendly with Jan. We work in very close proximity. She did confide in me.

RICHARD
I thought so. I think you convinced her to leave, that day. Jan has always been very susceptible to suggestion. I called it "weak brain." What did you tell her?

MADDIE
I am starting to feel very uncomfortable Mr... Officer. I think I'd like to stop now.

OFFICER
Of course. You are perfectly within your rights to do so. But no one is accusing anyone of anything. The medical examiner has been provided with the circumstances of the case. Until they sign the official death certificate confirming accidental death, the detectives at the scene, which unfortunately I was one of, must proceed to rule out a suspicious death. This was my first time seeing a deceased person, other than my own grandparents, and at least they were in a coffin. It was a horrendous scene, worse than anything I ever saw in the movies, and it's our responsibility to find the reason for it. I don't like pissing people off, but sadly– all in a day's work. You understand, I hope?

MADDIE
May I go?

OFFICER
Of course. Here is my card if you think of anything that might help us.

MADDIE takes the card. She looks at RICHARD.

MADDIE
Is it ok for me to take my things?

OFFICER
Personal items, yes.

RICHARD
I'm sorry, Maddie. I'm just under a lot of stress. I haven't slept. I haven't eaten. The shock... Of course, you did nothing to provoke this. Officer, I didn't mean to suggest... There is no way... Maddie was an exemplary employee. Everyone loved her, especially Jan. I did not mean to convey the impression that she was anything but.

MADDIE looks at RICHARD. She opens a drawer and swipes a handful of personal items into a bag. She shows them to the OFFICER who nods.

OFFICER
I'd like to reserve the right to question you another time. I'm sorry for the loss of your co-worker.

MADDIE
Thank you. I... I'm so sorry.

MADDIE exits. The OFFICER looks at RICHARD.

LIGHTS FADE
BLACKOUT

SCENE 6

MADDIE's apartment, later that evening. She is pacing about uncomfortably. The doorbell rings. She answers it. It's RICHARD. He is in a different shirt. He has cleaned up a bit. He is both relieved and anxious at the same time.

RICHARD
Oh my God! I am so sorry! Can you ever forgive me?

MADDIE
I'm glad you figured out my text. I know it was really cryptic. I used a friend's phone so you could always say it was a wrong number. I don't know if the police are checking your phone.

RICHARD
I don't know, either. Anything is possible. I was hoping you'd call. I felt terrible about the way things went this morning. And the day before. It's all such an awful mess. When you texted, "Swing by for a Paradise Mule on the house," I thought you meant the bar. I went to Kenny's first. I waited there for a bit, had a beer... wondered if it was some kind of set up. You're not wired, are you?

MADDIE
I am. Like crazy. Been so damn hyper. Just pacing, wondering. Was Charlie at the bar? I texted him. I didn't know how to tell you.

RICHARD
That was smart. I left my phone with him, just in case. You know, tracking... I almost didn't remember where you lived. That night, when I dropped you off, I remembered the Mexican restaurant next door. Tequila Mockingbird. Who could forget that?

MADDIE
You really put me in an awful position. Telling the truth felt like a lie, and I'm a terrible liar. I feel like I am in a James M. Cain novel.

RICHARD
I'm so sorry. I was beside myself. You were so angry at me. Justifiably. I was so out of line, and then to come home and find... It just broke me. And the detectives questioning me, when her body was still... I pulled her out. The water was cold. I knew it was probably too late but... Jan was the one who taught CPR training. I should have paid more attention. And then the detective, pummeling me with those questions, checking my computers, my private journals, I had written about you...

MADDIE
Oh my God. You didn't...

RICHARD
Not by name. I used... Carol. But they were asking me what Jan knew.

MADDIE
I know. I was there, remember? Richard... What happened?

RICHARD
It was a horrible fucking accident, with the worst timing possible.

MADDIE
Oh, was there better timing for you to have a dead wife?

RICHARD
That's not what I meant. It's just– Well, you know... I knew where Jan was all the time. Until yesterday. If I was home when she first fell, maybe I could have helped. You don't know the guilt I have about that. I had her phone. She couldn't even call me for help. I don't understand what was going on. Why would she be taking a bath? It was the middle of the afternoon.

MADDIE
Here's the thing, Richard. I know why.

RICHARD
How? Is your spidey sense telling you something?

MADDIE
Not my spidey sense. My movie geek fixation.

RICHARD
This is not some damn movie, Maddie, this is my life. What are you talking about?

MADDIE
Ok, normally, I only watch the old stuff. My dad used to say the only thing he liked that was produced after 1960 was me.

RICHARD
Ok, what does that have to do with–

MADDIE
Getting to that. So, occasionally I watch new movies, too. Gotta keep up to date. Ever hear of the Legally Blonde defense?

RICHARD
That's a new movie?

MADDIE
It was when I saw it in 2001. Anyway, in this movie, Elle Woods was able to catch the murderess because she said she was taking a shower after having a perm, and her hair was still curly. Water would have destroyed the perm salt.

RICHARD
This is not an episode of Columbo. The bath was full. Clearly, she slipped getting out. The towel rack was pulled off wall. What are you trying to say, Maddie? That I had something to do with this? Are you crazy?

MADDIE
I may be. That's why I wanted to talk to you first. Maybe you could clear things up. When Jan left, she said she was going to get a keratin

MADDIE (cont.)
treatment. Something she always wanted, but you said it was an extravagance.

RICHARD
Such an unnecessary expense. Who was she doing it for? I liked her hair the way it was.

MADDIE
She was doing it for herself. It's her money. Her hair. But here's the thing, Richard. She really wanted this. When you get a keratin treatment, and the medical examiner will know if she had, you absolutely cannot wash your hair for 72 hours. It ruins the whole process. Jan wouldn't have spent money on a treatment if she was just going to come home and ruin it.

RICHARD
Maybe she thought better of it once she got home.

MADDIE
I didn't tell anyone. I thought you might offer some kind of explanation.

RICHARD
This feels like one of your movie scenarios, Maddie, where the two lovers turn on each other.

MADDIE
Please, Richard, prove me wrong. Ease my conscience. I did kinda talk Jan into leaving yesterday. I talked to her about taking some control over her own life.

RICHARD
Looks like she may have done just that.

MADDIE
She said–

RICHARD
She said. She said... I don't know what she told you. But there are always two sides to every story.

MADDIE
Three, if you include the truth.

RICHARD
My conscience is clear, Maddie. I can come up with an explanation. But I don't think you're gonna like it. My wife just died, and you asked me up to your apartment. Maybe you want the detectives to think we're in this together, but that's not gonna work. I can account for my time. Can you? Maybe you killed Jan!

MADDIE
That's absurd, Richard. I had no reason to hurt her.

RICHARD
She was standing in the way of us being together. You knew I loved you. That I still love you...

MADDIE
What?

RICHARD
Sure, you hear about this all the time. The other woman. Amy Fisher thought she was doing a favor for that Buttafuoco guy. I told you how unhappy I was. How our love had died. Maybe after work, you made a little visit to the house, dragged her into the bathroom, hit her with something. I don't know. Maybe the hairdryer. Pushed her backwards into the tub, making sure her head hit the spigot, filled up the tub and pulled the towel rack down to make it look like an accident.

MADDIE
Except for one thing. Jan was naked. How could I have convinced her to take off her clothes? You are not making sense. You are crazy.

RICHARD
You are making me crazy! I don't want to make this a "he said, she said" business. She slipped in the tub. It was an accident. Can you just leave it at that? In a few months when this is all over, maybe we can both start fresh...

MADDIE
What? Richard, if you hurt her because of me, I couldn't live with that.

RICHARD
Fuckin' hair treatment. Who the hell would believe such a crazy story?

MADDIE
You're right. It's crazy. I shouldn't have brought it up.

RICHARD
No, you shouldn't have. Because now I am going to have a hard time trusting you, Maddie, and that's going to be very hard on me. All good relationships rely on trust. I would have done anything for you, for us... and it breaks my heart that I can't trust you.

MADDIE
You can trust me.

RICHARD
Nah, it will never be the same. I won't be able to let you out of my sight. Even after they determine it was an accident, which they will, at some point, you could decide your conscience is getting to you. That you'd be remiss if you didn't disclose some little tidbit to that young attractive detective. Doesn't matter how long you kept your sweet rosebud mouth shut. There is no statute of limitations on murder. I would never feel safe!

MADDIE
You know me, Richard. For weeks, I kept your... ok, our secret. I never cracked. Not once.

RICHARD
Now there is a crack in the wall. Something could seep through. I have to stop it. Seal the crack.

MADDIE
What are you saying? Oh, my God. You didn't! Tell me you didn't!

RICHARD
You're going to get what you wanted, movie queen. That scene at the end where the guy tells her how he did it. Didn't you learn anything from watching all those movies? You don't fall down in the woods when there is a maniac chasing you, and you should never be alone with the man you think is a killer.

MADDIE
Shit.

MADDIE tries to run for the door. RICHARD stops her.

RICHARD
For a smart girl, you can be really, really stupid. Ok, Nancy Drew, you want truth? I asked Ian if he would mind staying late, look over all the files you left from your hasty and dramatic departure. Yeah. Everyone saw that! Everyone felt real bad for me, so when I went back into my office and slammed the door, no one would think to bother me. I climbed out on the fire escape to the next office – unoccupied, fortunately – and down the back stairwell. I was home before Jan was. The look on her face was priceless. I bet Jan thought you told. Ha! Fitting. Betrayed by the only friend she thought she had. She told me she had gone to the bank, was thinking of moving her money around. She could clean me out. It's bad enough living off a woman's money, no real man does that, But, where would I be without it? Where would WE be? That was the moment I snapped. Where would she get an idea like that, Maddie? Somebody had to put that notion into her empty head.

MADDIE
I just thought... I'm so sorry...

RICHARD
Jan was surprised that I wasn't angry. I was as sweet as pie. Told her I loved the hair. That I was sorry about everything. That things would be different from now on. I didn't give a rat's ass about the money; it was her I wanted to hold on to. She melted into my arms. She'd been waiting to hear that for so long. I told her I was going to make love to her like it was a second honeymoon. Brought her a glass of champagne... Ok, it had a few of her anti-depressants in it. She was giddy, quivering in my arms, as I carried her to the bedroom. I don't think she even felt it when I banged her head on the headboard.

MADDIE
Oh, my God!

RICHARD
Shut up! I carried her into the bathroom. She might have been unconscious, or just super confused, not sure. I ran the bathwater. I took her hands and pulled down the towel rack, and then I pushed her backwards. There was a loud crack. That's when the blood mixed with the water and I knew I had her. I brought her clothes into the bathroom. Put back on my clothes, wiped down the headboard, and left the house. No one saw me. I was careful. Back into the office through the window. Ian was still pouring over the files and cursing you for leaving. I came out of my office around 7, and told Ian to go home, and that I would do the same. Perfect alibi. It appears all roads lead to you, my little Maddie. Checkmate. When that attractive detective finds you, he will put two and two together. Such a pity. We really would have made a great team.

RICHARD pulls out a pill vial. Shakes it.

RICHARD
Doxepin. You must have felt guilty. Get some water.

MADDIE
I'm not very thirsty.

RICHARD
Get it. Your hands need to be on the glass, so get it.

MADDIE crosses to the kitchen. RICHARD follows her.

MADDIE
I got it. I got it.

OFFICER enters.

OFFICER
We got it, too. All on tape. You ok, Ms. McKenzie?

MADDIE
No, I am not ok! You couldn't come out a little sooner? Holy shit!

OFFICER
We needed to be sure. Besides, you never said the panic word.

MADDIE
I fucking forgot the panic word!

RICHARD
This is entrapment. I asked you if you were wired.

MADDIE
And I answered. I said I was, and hyper. You misunderstood. And besides, I'm not a cop. I can lie.

RICHARD
You scheming, deceptive little bitch.

OFFICER
(Placing cuffs on RICHARD)
You have the right to remain silent.
(to MADDIE)
This is my first arrest! This is pretty exciting.

OFFICER (cont.)
(Back to RICHARD)
You have the right to remain silent. Anything you say can and will be used against you in a court of law. You have the right to an attorney. If you cannot afford an attorney, one will be provided for you. Do you understand the rights I have just told you?

RICHARD
I fucking know my rights. And now that I am looking at you again, you are not that attractive.
(to MADDIE)
Wherever I go, know that you played a part in this, Maddie. You will have to live with the fact that you had a hand in Jan's death. Yeah. Live with that, you devious, manipulative shrew. She's dead because of YOU.

MADDIE
(to OFFICER)
Now you see why I don't date.

The OFFICER leads RICHARD out of the apartment.

OFFICER
We'll be in touch, Ms. Mckenzie. And thank you.

MADDIE
I think I need a drink.

RICHARD
You don't drink!

MADDIE
I may start!

MADDIE slams the door, and does some deep breathing. She goes to the fridge and looks for something. There is no alcohol. She gets out a tub of ice cream and a coke, and goes to the TV.

She sits on the couch, blankly eating the ice cream. She turns on the TV. The theme music for DOUBLE INDEMNITY comes on.

MADDIE
Oh, hell!

She turns off the TV. Sits for a moment. Picks up the phone and dials, as she slowly starts crying.

MADDIE
Hello, mommy? Yeah... I'm ok. Actually, I'm not. I just... I need my mommy. Can you... Ok... Thanks... Chocolate... Yeah, I'm breathing. It's a long story.

LIGHTS SLOWLY FADE
END OF SCENE

EPILOGUE

MADDIE is back at Kenny's bar having been just served some cheese fries.

MADDIE
Thanks, Charlie. Nope, still filling out applications. Had a few interviews. It's hard when they ask you why you left your last job. Not even sure what I want to do now. I guess I'll have to be the new "new" me, since the old "new" me didn't work out so well. I was really trying to help that woman get out from under. Now she's six feet under, ten people are out of work, and I am the key witness in a murder trial that could go on for months. The movies. A blessing and a curse for me. I never stop and think what happens to everyone after the credits roll. Hey, maybe you could use a little help behind the bar? I mean, I don't know shit about mixing drinks, but I could really push the cheese fries. Best in the city!

The bar door opens and a MAN enters (can be played by the same person as OFFICER).

MAN
WOO!! Crazy weather out there. The wind is nuts! It's like that scene in "Mary Poppins" when all the nannies start flying away. Honestly, one lady almost lost her Yorkie! Nice place to wait it all out.

MAN walks up to the bar. Sees MADDIE.

MAN
I'll have a beer, and what she's having. I love cheese fries, though I am partial to disco fries. Fries with cheese and gravy.

Turns to MADDIE.

MAN
Ever try those?

MADDIE gathers up her things, leaving the uneaten cheese fries.

MADDIE
Put it on my tab, Charlie! See ya!

MADDIE runs towards the door.

MAN
Wait! You don't want to go outside now. It's practically a hurricane.

MADDIE exits slamming the door.

MAN
Wow! Some women are just crazy! Whatever you got on tap, man... and the fries.

MAN watches the door. The wind howls. The lights fade.

END OF PLAY

More plays by Bambi Everson

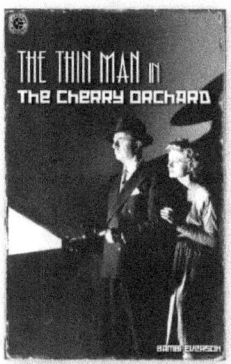

Visit BambiEverson.com

Also available in paperback

THE THIN MAN IN THE CHERRY ORCHARD

In this sardonic mashup, Dashiell Hammett's hard-boiled, glamorously pickled American sleuths, Nick and Nora Charles, meet their cousins, the stoic inhabitants of Chekhov's bleak Russian tundra. Naturally, a murder, and hilarity, ensues. Can Nick solve the crime before they run out of vodka? Full length, approximately 100 minutes, one optional intermission. Comedy-Mystery. 4M, 4F.

Also available in paperback

NICK AND NORA GO OFF-BROADWAY

In this standalone sequel to The Thin Man in the Cherry Orchard, Anya convinces Nora to take part in an amateur theater production. As is par for the course, a murder takes place and Nick must solve the crime before opening night. Full length, approx. 100m, one intermission. Comedy-Mystery, 5M, 3F.

Also available in paperback

FINDING ANDREW
Twelve-year-old Virginia's peculiar connection to Andrew is met with uncertainty and doubt by her best friend, Max. One act, approximately 22 minutes. Drama. 1F, 2 teens (M/F)

DAD'S HOME
Paul is home from the office. Something is terribly wrong, and everybody knows but him. One act, approximately 50 minutes. Drama. 2M, 1F, 1M teen.

Also available in paperback

SINCERELY HELD BELIEFS

Mandy is caught between her two friends. One a grieving mother, and the other a zealous clairvoyant who is convinced she is receiving messages from the other side. Mandy must try to mediate these two relationships, while staying true to her own beliefs. Full length, approximately 80 minutes. Psychological Drama. 3F, 20s-40s. Trigger warning: child death.

Also available in paperback

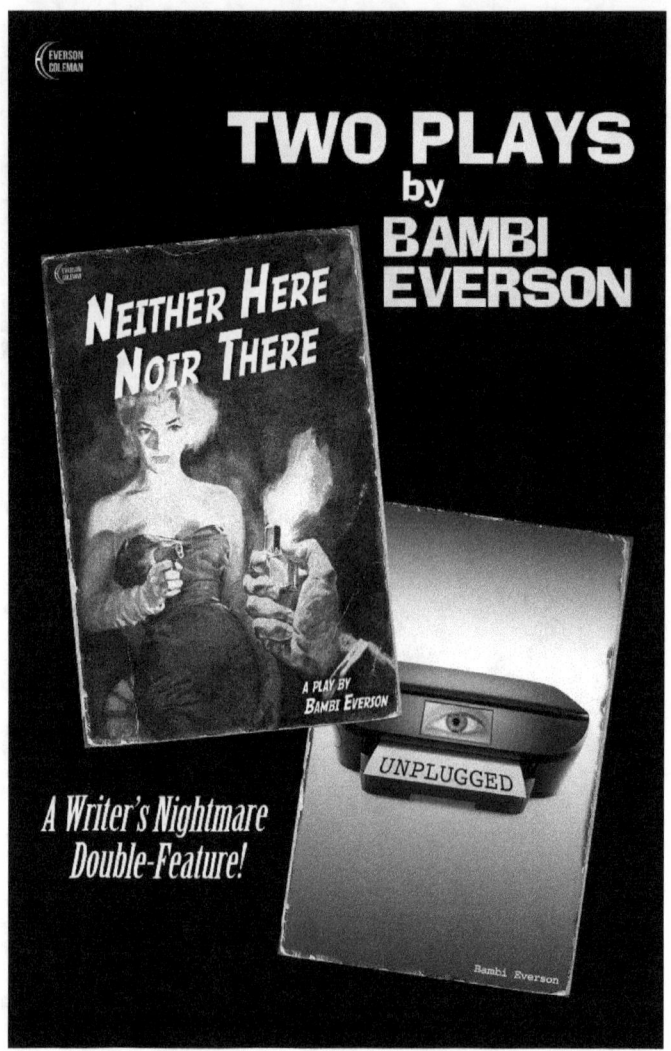

NEITHER HERE NOIR THERE
Michael, newly divorced, has taken up residence with his best friend, Alice. He begins to rework a discarded film noir novel, but soon his femme fatale, Maxie Malone, comes to life with an agenda of her. *Blithe Spirit* meets *The Maltese Falcon*. Full length, approx. 60 minutes. Comedy. 2F, 1M.

UNPLUGGED
A writer's work is disrupted when his printer takes on a life, and an agenda, of its own. One act, approx. 50 minutes. Dark comedy. 2F, 2M.

Bambi Everson

ABOUT THE AUTHOR

Bambi Everson is an actor, teaching artist, and the author of over 30 plays. Her full-length, THE THIN MAN IN THE CHERRY ORCHARD had a sold out run at the 2019 New York Fringe Festival, and is available in paperback from The Drama Book Shop (NYC) and Amazon, along with a growing list of volumes.

MURDER IS SERVED won 2nd Place in the 2019 One Act competition at The Little Theatre of Alexandria, VA. NEITHER HERE NOIR THERE had a sold out run at Manhattan Repertory Theatre in 2017. It also received a student production at Winthrop University in Rock Hill, S.C. In 2015, she was the recipient of the Yip Harburg Foundation scholarship and her work has been produced at Emerging Artists Theatre and at Hudson Guild.

She's been influenced as much by cinema as she has by theater, an inescapable accident of birth, as she's the daughter of noted film historian, William K. Everson.

Bambi teaches playwriting in Manhattan arts schools, and is a member of The Dramatists Guild, and Actors' Equity Association.

Follow her adventures at her website, bambieverson.com

www.ingramcontent.com/pod-product-compliance
Lightning Source LLC
LaVergne TN
LVHW051840080426
835512LV00018B/2980